Knifemaking
with Bob Loveless

By Durwood Hollis

Published by

Gun Digest® Books, an imprint of Caribou Media Group, LLC

Gun Digest Media
5600 W. Grande Market Drive, Suite 100
Appleton, WI 54913
www.gundigest.com

To order books or other products call 920.471.4522
or visit us online at www.gundigeststore.com

ISBN-13: 978-1-4402-1155-3

Edited by Corrina Peterson
Cover Design by Tom Nelsen
Interior Design by Dave Hauser
Front cover photos by Jim Weyer, Toledo

Printed in the United States of America

10 9 8 7 6 5 4 3 2

WE ARE
HONORED

1929 ~ 2010

Just as this book was going to the printer, we received the sad news that Bob Loveless, a member of the Blade Magazine Cutlery Hall Of Fame©, had passed away on Sept. 2, 2010. The father of the modern custom knife movement, the man who popularized the dropped hunter, Big Bear sub-hilt fighter and other knives, and, along with Richard Barney, co-wrote *How To Make Knives*, the precursor to this book, was gone.

In 1999, I had the privilege of visiting Bob in his shop in Riverside, California, to conduct an interview for *BLADE*® *Magazine*. The thing that stood out was the cleanliness of both the shop and the man himself. Like the lines of his knives, Loveless and his shop were clean, un-cluttered and unpre-tentious. Though he wore a blue denim shirt out over his blue jeans, he was clean-shaven and his clothes were spotless. The ease with which he answered my questions belied a shop and per-sonal appear-ance that—sans the untucked shirt—would have passed most any military inspection. At one point he even grabbed a push broom and swept up some miniscule bits of dirt unseen to all but his discerning eye. Whether it was his polite way of telling me the in-terview was running long or he simply was that fastidious, I don't know. I do know that he had a sign on the wall that read, "Your mother does not work here. Please pick up after yourself."

We at *BLADE* and F+W Media are humbled and proud to present this work showcasing the knifemaking legacy of Mr. Loveless. Though knifemaking was but one of many pursuits that made this fascinating man tick, it is what he will be remembered for most.

We are honored to be able to add to the memories.

Steve Shackleford
Editor
BLADE

From the Author

DURWOOD HOLLIS

THIS WORK IS DEDICATED TO
MY FRIEND AND KNIFE MAKER
LOYD THOMSEN.

Loyd owns a ranch in the prairie country of South Dakota, where
he raises cattle, feuds with coyotes and makes knives. Good friends
are hard to come by. When you find such an individual, they become a
part of your own extended family. So it has been with Loyd Thomsen.
Thank you Loyd for who you are and your continued friendship.

[ACKNOWLEDGEMENTS]

The scope of this book was such that without Bob Loveless it would have never come to fruition. Throughout the course of several interviews, Bob was the consummate gentleman. Never growing impatient with my seemingly endless string of questions, he answered every inquiry with experience birthed out of more than half a century of knife making. Certainly, Bob Loveless is well worthy of my gratitude.

Likewise, I am thankful to knife maker and Loveless partner Jim Merritt for his insight into the career of a man who's become a legend in the world of handmade knives. There's no doubt that his long association with Bob Loveless has given rise to a true friendship between them.

I am also indebted to Utah-based knife maker Steve Johnson for sharing with me the time he worked with Loveless in the early 1970s. During our conversation about that relationship, you could hear the warmth in his voice when he said, "Bob treated me like a son."

Montana knife maker Steven Kelly is also deserving of my thanks. Steve was a consultant on several of the chapters of this book and his unselfish assistance was a tremendous contribution to this effort.

Loveless knife collector and purveyor John Denton provided many of the images contained herein. Those images gave life to my words and served as a window to Bob Loveless' knife making career. For his generosity and kindness, I will be forever grateful.

I am also grateful to photographer Hiro Soga for allowing me to use many of his fine photos in this book. His stunning work clearly illuminates the purity and clean lines of a Bob Loveless creation.

Of course there are others who contributed to getting this book into print. Steve Shackleford, editor, and Joe Kertzman, managing editor of BLADE Magazine, worked behind the scenes at F+W Media/Krause Publications to "get the ball rolling." I truly appreciate the confidence and support of both men.

Lastly, Corrina Peterson, Editor, Firearms/Outdoor Books at F+W Media/Krause Publications encouraged me when things bogged down. I most certainly give thanks for her support and patience.

And a special "thank you" goes out to my wife Anita for putting up with the mess in my office during the months that this project was underway. This book has truly been a difficult taskmaster, but knowing that it will be found in the resource library of many future knife makers is a reward of uncountable measure.

[ABOUT THE AUTHOR]

Since childhood, Durwood Hollis has been regularly involved in outdoor pursuits. Game meals were a staple on the dinner table in camp and at home, and a sharp knife was key to proper game care. Durwood's first cutlery mentor was his father, who taught him knife safety, sharpening and field use.

For nearly 35 years, his writing has appeared in a wide range of outdoor magazines, including Outdoor Life, Petersen's Hunting Magazine, Guns and Ammo, Gun World, Tactical Knives, BLADE Magazine *and* Boar Hunter.

Over the course of his freelance writing career, Durwood served as the editorial director for The Complete Book of Knives *(Petersen's Publications, 1985); and authored the* Complete Game Care Guide *(Brunton/Lakota, 1995);* Elk: Strategies for the Hunter *(Krause Publication, 2001);* The Complete Book of Hunting Knives *(Krause Publications, 2001);* Hunting Monster Mule Deer in Arizona's Kaibab Region *(Arizona Big Game Hunting, 2001);* Hunting North American Big Game *(Krause Publications, 2002) and* Hunting Upland Game & Waterfowl *(Krause Publications, 2003).*

A lifelong resident of southern California, the father of six children and grandfather of a dozen grandchildren, the author resides near Los Angeles with his wife Anita and their youngest daughter Kailea.

Photo by Jim Weyer, Toledo

Table of Contents

Foreword

BY A.G. RUSSELL

In 1964, I started a small mail order business selling Arkansas sharpening stones through tiny ads in gun magazines like *American Rifleman* and *Guns & Ammo*. Very quickly, I began to sell knives in those ads as well. Sometime in 1967, I made a trip to sit down face to face with the handmade knifemakers I had come to know as a result of this new business. One of those makers was D.E. "Ed" Henry in Mountain Ranch, California. Ed had a small knife collection and on the evening of my visit, I was thoroughly enjoying the opportunity to examine those knives up close and personal. After looking at several nice pieces, I picked up a knife that I did not recognize, and I kid you not, the hair at the back of my neck lifted as I looked at the most stunning fighting knife I had ever seen. The mark was "R.W. Loveless, Lawndale, CA."

I asked Ed, "Who is R.W. Loveless?" He refused to tell me anything unless I agreed that I would not provide any promotion for Loveless. I told Ed I could not make such a promise and he finally gave in, telling me that he and Loveless had traded knives. During that time most knifemakers were envious of each other and Ed Henry was no exception. He did not want me to use my little company and my contact with gun writers to promote Loveless.

After my visit with Ed, I went on to the San Francisco airport and called R.W. Loveless. I was surprised to learn that he knew who I was and that he was quite excited to hear from me. He insisted on picking me up at the Los Angeles airport that afternoon. Bob and I spent hours talking knives and the knife business. We formed a friendship that, even after more than 40 years and being separated by half the country, endures to this day.

Bob and I talked endlessly on the phone, working to promote his business and knifemakers in general. One of the results of this was the formation of the Knifemakers' Guild in 1970. In the beginning, the only support we could find came from Dan Dennehy. Most makers were afraid that others would steal their customers. The Guild became very important to knifemakers and managed to stay relevant for the next 40 years. Bob always wanted to expand knowledge of knifemaking to as many as he could, so he was always free with information about materials and techniques.

R.W. (Bob) Loveless is universally acknowledged as the greatest designer of hunting and combat knives in the entire history of our industry. His designs are copied and adapted by other makers all over the world.

I have no doubt that Bob's designs will endure as long as people use hunting knives and wish to carry boot and combat knives. Not many people have even a small hope that their name will endure for 100 years after their death. Bob surely can.

A.G. Russell
Rogers, Arkansas

Preface

Most writers find it difficult to encapsulate the life and contributions of any individual in the pages of a book. Even the best attempts fall short of the actual reality. At best, only a representation can be presented and even that only touches on a few elements of a life. That which is revealed in print only hints at the vast substance that remains beyond the immediate. The same thing can be said of this tome.

When a man like Robert "Bob" Waldorf Loveless has lived more than eight decades, only the peaks of his life and work can be seen above the clouds of the past. Most of the valleys remain in dim mists beyond remembrance. However, when compared with what is seen and recalled, that which is overlooked or forgotten is of far less importance. In this instance, that which is timeless remains in steel. And that alone speaks of the man who gave it life.

For more than half-a-century, Bob Loveless has made his mark in the arena of handmade knives. He emerged onto the scene in an era where there were few notable knife makers. Men like Bo Randall, Harry Morseth, Rudy Ruana and later Bill Moran were the most prominent figures in that early era of knife making.

My first encounter with Bob Loveless came about when he had a shop in Lawndale, California, a small suburb south of downtown Los Angeles. And from time-to-time, I would see him at an occasional knife show. Many years afterward, I was asked to present a seminar on knife work in the field at the BLADE Show West, held at that time in Ontario, California. That's where I saw Bob once again.

Shortly after my seminar began, Bob walked into the room accompanied by Steve Shackleford, the editor of *BLADE* Magazine. I must admit, Bob's presence was a bit disconcerting. When he made comments during the seminar, I was more than just a little concerned. However, his statements were right on point. Always a gentleman, afterwards he came up to me, shook my hand and complimented me on the presentation.

Several more years ensued and Loveless continued to remain a bit of an enigma. It wasn't until I visited his Riverside, California, knife shop that a hint of who he was began to emerge. That particular visit happened at a time when Loveless was involved as a design consultant with a production knife firm.

"If a production knife company is able to produce a Loveless-style knife, with good steel, at an affordable price, then that allows the average guy to own one of my designs at an affordable price," Bob said.

After that, I visited the Loveless shop on a few more occasions. And the idea of writing a book about his life and knife making career began to germinate. When I approached Bob about the book, he was quite positive about the idea. Subsequently, he granted me the necessary access to produce such an undertaking.

I was aware that a couple of other books had included some commentary on Bob Loveless and his work. However, things change over time, new materials emerge and knife making methodologies evolve. In this effort it is my goal to update and expand on what has already been written about Bob Loveless and his knife building techniques.

In the pages ahead, you'll read about Bob Loveless the man, his life and his work. You'll also be able to follow him through various phases of knife building, from raw steel stock to the finished product, including material about how-to make a sheath for your new knife. There are chapters on knife making tools, blade sharpening, knife care and upkeep and a helpful resource guide. In addition, there are many illustrative images, including several Loveless knife images that have never been published previously. A lot more lies ahead, so read on and enjoy.

Durwood Hollis
Rancho Cucamonga, California 2010

CHAPTER ONE

The Loveless Story

FROM A HUMBLE BEGINNING ON A FARM, ROBERT "BOB" W. LOVELESS HAS RISEN TO THE PINNACLE OF KNIFE MAKING

When it comes to writing a biographical sketch, where to begin is not always as clear as many would believe. Some would pick a seminal event that had a transforming effect on the life of the individual in question. Still others would begin at the moment of birth. When selecting a point of origin to begin the life story of R. W. "Bob" Loveless, the very same challenge beset this writer. And to fully understand the life any individual, I believe one must start with their parents. Therefore, it's at that point that this story begins.

Bob's father, Carl B. Loveless was born in 1890 and served in World War I. Returning home from the war Carl brought with him the scars of conflict. Like many others that saw duty at the battle front, his lungs were badly damaged by the mustard gas attacks unleashed by the Germans, and breathing difficulties would beset him for the rest of his life. Looking for the quiet life of a small town, Carl settled in Warren, Ohio, where he met and married Doris B. Huff. At the time of this union Carl was in his late 30s and his bride was barely out of her teens. While initially the age difference didn't seem to be a factor, in time both partners found themselves looking for something different in the marriage. Only a couple of years passed before Carl and Doris were divorced. However, one significant event in the marriage did occur, the birth of a son in 1929, Robert Waldorf Loveless.

America was just entering what is known as the Great Depression in the early 1930s and just making a living was difficult for most families, especially those that had

(above) Bob Loveless' maternal grandfather, Clinton Huff owned a small farm about halfway between Warren, Ohio, and Sharon, Pennsylvania. It was there that Bob spent much of his early life. (Image: Bob Loveless)

(right) Daisy Huff was Bob Loveless' maternal grandmother. She and her husband Clinton were responsible for teaching Bob self-reliance during the Great Depression. (Image: Bob Loveless)

(opposite) Bob Loveless has been making knives for nearly 60 years. His work has been widely copied and his influence felt throughout the cutlery industry, from production factories to handmade knives. He characterizes his knives as "everything a knife should be, and nothing else." (Image: Durwood Hollis)

suffered a divorce. Sent to live with his maternal grandparents, Clinton and Daisy Huff, young Bob found himself on their small (17 acre) farm in Vienna Township, located about halfway between Warren and Sharon, Pennsylvania.

Remembering that time, Bob said, "Like everybody else during the Depression, we had hard time just surviving. My grandparents raised chickens and we ate eggs, lots of eggs. We grew a mix of crops on the farm, including a little tobacco, some rhubarb and berries. We were fortunate enough to have a cow, so milk, cream and butter was never a problem. And there was garden and plenty of wild game in the surrounding woods."

After the divorce, Bob's father continued to work as a delivery driver in Warren. Unfortunately, Carl fell in with some unsavory individuals which lead to his participation in a burglary of a Railway Express safe. It didn't take too long for the police to catch up with Carl and his partners and they were sentenced to prison terms. After his release from confinement, it seemed that Carl was never really the same. He drank heavily and his health continued to slowly erode. In 1977, he died of esophageal cancer.

Remembering his father, Bob said, "He was sweet old man. All he ever wanted was to settle down, get married and enjoy life. Sadly, a combination of alcohol and his breathing disorder seemed to wear him down. While he wasn't a big influence on my life, I still remember him with fondness."

When Bob was eight years old, his grandfather Clinton died. Afterwards, he went to live with his mother in town. "It seemed to me that all she wanted to do was go out every night and have fun. Eventually, she remarried twice, but she never had any other children. In reality, my mother was absent much of the time," Bob said.

The one thing that this experience taught Bob was self-reliance. Five years after his grandfather's death, Bob began spending a lot of his spare time at a small airfield near Warren. It didn't take long for him to convince the owner that swapping odd jobs for flight instruction would be good training for the young teenager. While the owner, Ernie Hall, taught Bob the basics of flying, he wasn't about to let a fourteen-year-old kid take a plane up on his own. Not to be deterred, Bob waited until Ernie was away from the field one day. Sensing an opportunity to fly solo, Bob jumped into the owner's Piper J-3

Cub and took off.

"While I was aloft, I saw Ernie's Studebaker returning back to the field. As fast as I could, I landed the plane and pulled it up to the hanger. Even though Ernie knew I'd been up in the plane all by myself, he only asked me how things went. After I told him everything went fine, he simple walked away and never mentioned my solo exploit again," Bob said.

Airplanes, particularly bi-planes, are still a Loveless passion. Over the years he has owned four amateur-built, single-seat biplanes. In 1983, Bob crashed one of the planes at a Riverside airfield. "I was coming in for a landing and another pilot who wasn't flying the landing pattern got in my blind spot. My propeller hit his plane and we both went down. While both of us managed to walk away from the mishap, the tibia in my left leg was broken and that put me out of commission for about three months," Bob said. Despite this experience, Bob continued to fly until 1989.

Bob Loveless' mother, Doris B. Huff, was still barely out of her teens when she married Bob's father, Carl B. Loveless. While the marriage was short-lived, the union produced a son, Robert Waldorf Loveless, in 1929. (Image: Bob Loveless)

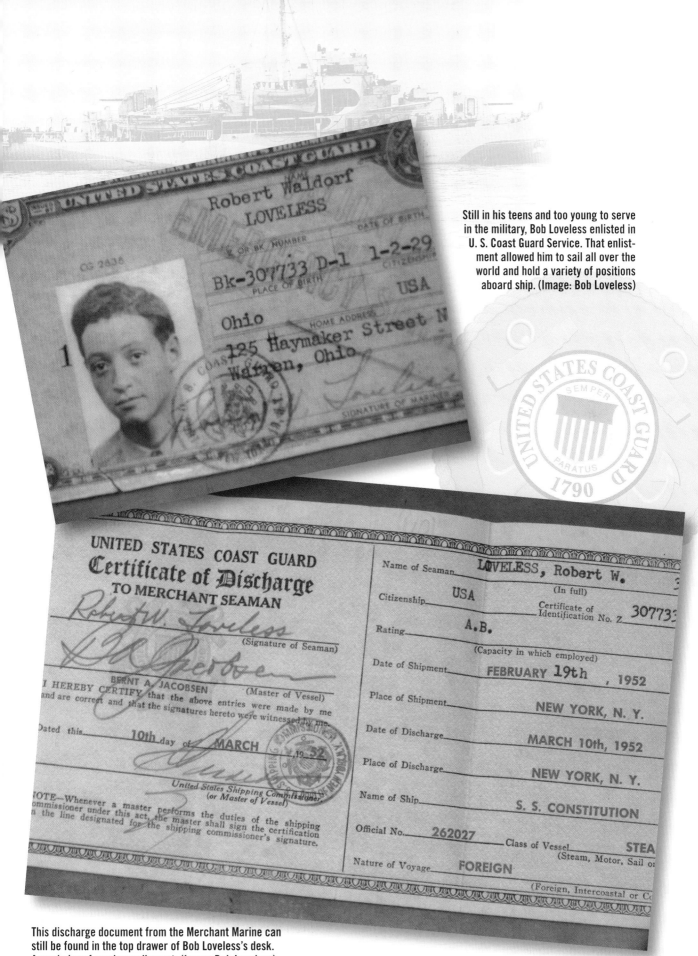

Still in his teens and too young to serve in the military, Bob Loveless enlisted in U. S. Coast Guard Service. That enlistment allowed him to sail all over the world and hold a variety of positions aboard ship. (Image: Bob Loveless)

This discharge document from the Merchant Marine can still be found in the top drawer of Bob Loveless's desk. A reminder of service well spent. (Image Bob Loveless)

World War II was well under way by the time Bob Loveless hit his teen years. Too young to enlist in the military, he made a discreet adjustment to his birth certificate and joined the Merchant Marine. During the course of his career aboard ship, he sailed to more ports than he can recall as a Deck Hand, Able Seaman, Coal Passer and Yeoman Seaman.

Shortly after the war, on his 17th birthday, Loveless joined the Army Air Corps and was given a two-year stint in the Pacific on Guam and Iwo Jima. He didn't fly while in the Air Corps, but he did work the air traffic control tower on Iwo Jima. Later on, he finished his tour of duty at Wright-Patterson Air Force Base, near Dayton, Ohio. Finally, he was discharged from the service in 1948.

During his time at Wright-Patterson, Bob made the decision to enroll in the Institute of Design in Chicago, Illinois. Even though he wasn't a high school graduate (he had earned a GED), he was accepted to the school based on drawings he had done while in the Army Air Corps.

"It seemed to me that everyone at the Institute was only interested in designing commercial centers, while my interests lie with more practical architecture. What really stirred my thought processes were things like single-family homes and mobile homes. Without any meaningful encouragement from my instructors, I just up and quit school," Bob said.

Shortly afterwards, Bob enrolled in Kent State University in Ohio. "I definitely wasn't the average college freshman. My knowledge of the workings of the English language wasn't up to par, but I could express myself. And I was an avid reader. One of things you acquire from reading is a basic knowledge of the English language. That knowledge will be exhibited in straightforward writing. To be successful, a man needs to possess both logic and an extensive vocabulary," Bob said.

While his stint at Kent State only lasted a couple of quarters, the experience did stimulate his intellectual interests. However, he quickly grew tired of campus life and returned once

Bob Loveless' Continuous Discharge Book indicates that he was living in Warren, Ohio, in 1950. The photo in the book was taken when he was barely 21 years old. (Image: Bob Loveless)

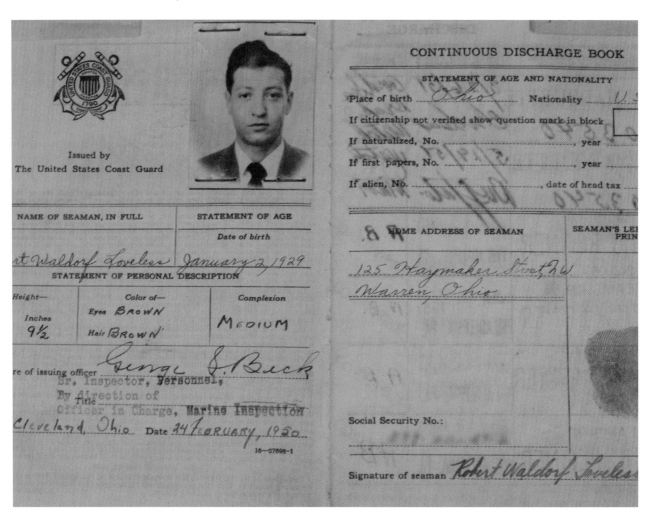

This is an example of one of Bob's very first knives that was made for Abercrombie & Fitch in New York City during the early 1950s. (Image: John Denton)

again to the Merchant Marine. For a time, Bob worked on bulk carriers plying Great Lakes waters. Seeking a greater measure of stability, he finally ended up on an oiler that went to various ports on the East Coast.

In 1953, while working on the Sun Oil Company tanker the Passaic Sun, Loveless read an article in True magazine about knife maker Bo Randall. "Knives were used on a daily basis aboard ship. After reading about Randall's knives and how well they stood up to abuse, I decided I wanted one," Bob said

On his day off, Loveless went to the Abercrombie & Fitch store in downtown Manhattan, New York. At the time, Abercrombie & Fitch was the preferred outdoor gear establishment of discriminating sportsmen. President Teddy Roosevelt had shopped there before traipsing off on his African safari. Likewise, Hollywood film star Clark Gable and author Ernest Hemmingway made regular visits the store. Abercrombie & Fitch as a retail sporting goods entity is no more (Abercrombie still operates as a youth-oriented clothing chain in many major cities). At that time, however, the store carried everything a outdoorsmen could need, from the finest camping gear to handmade English shotguns. If there was a Randall knife to be had, young Loveless thought that he could find it there.

"I am certain that my oil-stained denims, pee coat and watch cap didn't really make me the typical Abercrombie & Fitch customer," Bob recalled. He was promptly met by a rather snippy sales person that seemed to consider Loveless not the type of customer he was used to serving. When Bob asked to look at a Randall knife, the clerk told him that "We simply don't have any. And it will take at least nine months to get one."

When asked about the experience, Bob said, "The clerk didn't even ask if I wanted to put my name on the waiting list for a Randall knife. It was evident that he didn't want to be bothered with a young guy wearing the working clothes of a merchant seaman."

In his early 20s at the time, Bob Loveless might have been short in years, but he was long in worldly experience. Unable to acquire the knife he wanted, Bob decided that he would make one of his own. Doing things himself was nothing new to Bob Loveless. Growing up on his grandparent's farm during the economic woes of the Depression had taught him self-reliance. Toys were costly and the money to purchase them hard to come by. If you wanted something to play with, you had to make it yourself out of whatever you could scrounge. Scrap wood could be fashioned into a toy gun, a piece of tin doing service as the hammer, trigger and trigger guard, with a little blue ink providing a touch of realism.

On his return to the ship, Bob passed a huge junk yard. "I told the taxi driver to stop and let me out. I rea-

soned that automotive springs would make a good knife and I wanted get some pieces from the junk yard. One of the workers at the yard took a torch and cut four or five pieces of spring steel for me out of a 1937 Packard. Back at the ship I rough ground the steel to the shape I wanted. Working in my spare time, it probably took me a week to get the knife finished," Bob said.

Cutting out a blade blank, putting a handle on and finishing it was one thing; heat treating the steel was something else altogether. Bob heated the blade up on the ship's galley stove until it was "cherry-red." He then plunged the blade into a five-gallon bucket of refrigerate oil. All of the scale easily fell off and the knife came out a dull gray color. "The knife looked pretty good to me," Bob said.

Bob didn't know about tempering, and the heat treatment he had applied to the blade had made it so hard that it was unable to withstand contact abuse and started chipping. "The blade cut well enough for a short time, but then the edge started flaking away," Bob said.

The Chief Engineer aboard the ship suggested that the solution to the problem lay in the hardness imparted by the initial heat treatment. Reading up on heat treatment of metals in a local public library, Bob was determined to solve the blade edge problem. Taking the knife handle off, he placed the blade on a copper plate that had been heated on the galley stove. It didn't take too long for

This is a close-up image of the Abercrombie & Fitch marking that Bob placed on each knife that was delivered to that firm. (Image: John Denton)

the blade to turn dark blue, a sure sign that some of the hardness had been drawn out of the steel.

"My approach to heat treatment wasn't very scientific or even well-experienced. Even so, it worked. The change in blade edge performance was tremendous and the knife turned out to be a great cutting tool," Bob said.

Loveless Knife Sells for $250,000

At the Chicago Custom Knife Show, held September 7-8, 2008, a sub-hilt Bowie made by Bob Loveless in 1957 sold for a reported $250,000. The sale price for the engraved "Delaware Maid" Bowie was the most ever paid for a Loveless knife. The knife was initially sold by Loveless in 1959 for $350. "I had to sell it for grocery money," Loveless said.

Made from Jessop 139B nickel-alloy steel, the knife features hidden tang construction and an ivory handle. The hilt, sub-hilt and pommel are all crafted from sterling silver. The name plate is gold and the parry strip atop the back of the blade is brass. The engraving on the knife and the carving on the ivory handle was done by Francis Monoghan. The blade is marked "The Delaware Maid" directly above the words "Bowie Fighting Knife." Also marked on the blade is the name of the maker, "R. W. Loveless," and the point of production origin "Claymont, Del."

Determined to show up the clerk at Abercrombie & Fitch that had "looked down his nose at him," Bob returned to the store with knife in hand. However, satisfaction was not to come. Abercrombie had wisely terminated the clerk's employment. However, the floor manager looked at Bob's recent edged creation and liked it well enough to order four more just like it. When Bob had completed work on the knives, he returned to the store and the manager promptly paid him $14.00 for each one.

"Needless to say, I was excited about that sale. So much so that, before leaving the store, I spent every cent right on the spot," Bob said.

Impressed with his workmanship on the knives, the floor manager requested that Bob make more for the store. Bob was paid $20.70 for each knife and the store sold them for more than they got for a Randall knife. "That made me real proud," Bob said.

With the purchase order from Ab-

ercrombie in hand, Bob went to the Claymont, Delaware, branch of Wilmington Trust and was able to obtain a personal loan for $1,000. He spent the bulk of the funds on tools, which included a grinder, an anvil, couple of vises, a drill, some files and a furnace for heat treating his blades. Working until the wee hours of the morning, Bob was able to build 72 knives in just 74 days. Not too bad, considering that he worked a full-time job during the day with Sun Oil on a relieving gang and stayed up half the night building knives.

Interestingly, should you find one of those very first Abercrombie-Loveless knives, you can expect to pay several thousand dollars for one, even if it isn't in top condition. While one of those originals may not be the Holy Grail of knives, it would be a treasured find for

This photo of Bob and two of his three daughters depicts a loving father with a girl in each arm. Taken at the Loveless home in Delaware, the entire family would eventually relocate to California. (Image: Bob Loveless)

any collector. When Loveless made several replicas of that first knife, bearing the name The 35th Anniversary Knife, the knives sold for $3,500 each. Who knows what an original would fetch on today's collectable knife market.

During his time at Kent State, Bob met Lenny George Leutzakis, who would eventually become his wife and the mother of his three daughters (Alison, Robin Ann and Mary Lisa Ann). To support his growing family, Bob left knife making for a few years and went to work for E. I. du Pont de Nemours & Company in Wilmington, Delaware, as a technician. However, he eventually returned to his cutlery trade.

During this period in his life, Bob was faced with several challenges, including a troubled marriage and illness within the family. When the Loveless family physician suggested that they move from Delaware to a drier, milder climate as a way of controlling the pneumonia that threatened one of his daughters, the family moved to Modesto, California. Arriving in California, Bob quickly found work at a machine shop and eventually set up a small shop of his own. His machine shop work continued until the late 1960s, when he supervised a shop with some 85 employees. All the while, Bob continued making knives.

Not long after they arrived in Modesto, Bob and his family moved once again to Lawndale, California. Bob set up shop in the garage next to the house, and by the time the 1970s approached, knife making was tak-

ing almost all of his time. "Once again, I worked a full-time job during the day and made knives at night," Bob said.

The Loveless home in Riverside, California, is small and unpretentious. The single feature of this property that compelled Bob to purchase it was the detached shop in the rear. (Image: Durwood Hollis)

In 1971, Bob's marriage ended and he moved to Riverside, California. The house he bought was small, but the property had a shop at the rear that was nearly as large as the main residence. "I wanted the property because of the shop. I was tired of working in a garage," Bob said.

In 1978, Bob remarried. His Japanese bride, Yoshiko Rich was born in Japan and had come to the United States as a very young woman. Like Bob she had also been previously married and had two grown daughters. The couple has remained together for 31 years.

Of course, Bob had help. Throughout the years there have been several apprentice knife makers in his shop. Steve Johnson, an accomplish knife maker who now lives in Utah, worked with him for a three years in the early 1970s. Toward the end of that decade, Koichiro Oda, a Japanese assistant, worked with Bob for awhile. And in 1983, Jim Merritt came on as Bob's assistant. "Jim is now a full partner in the business and does most of the work," Bob said.

The Loveless knife making methodology has changed over the years. Initially, his first knives (the ones made from automobile springs) were forged. "No knife mak-

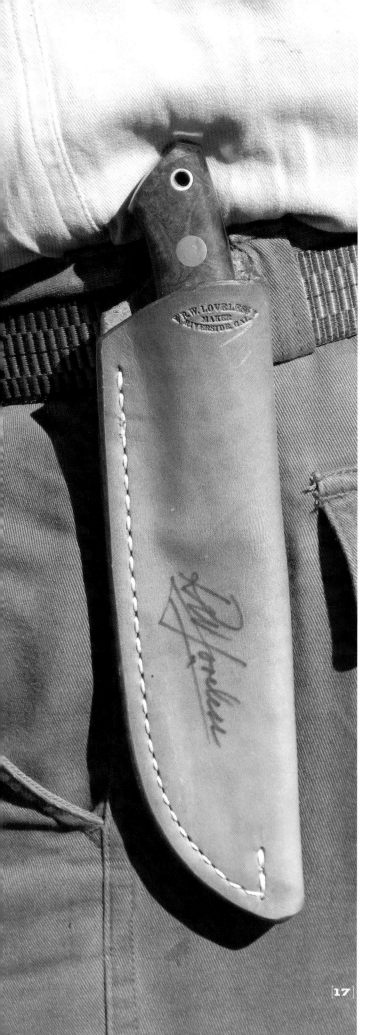

er can improve on steel made specifically for blades by steel manufacturers. I don't care how much you beat, twist, turn or freeze a piece of steel, you won't improve on what already has been improved upon. Forging is hard work and a poor way to shape metal. It's blacksmith work pure and simple. And not the best way to make a knife," Bob stated.

Even though one of Loveless' knives recently changed hands in a private sale for a reported $250,000, he'll quickly let you know that he doesn't make art knives. "I make knives for guys who want to use them," Bob said. While he has made boot knives, an occasional fighter and even a few knives with engraved bolsters, his primary knife making focus is on hunting knives, especially his fixed-blade, drop-point hunter design.

While Bob hunted as a youth and young man, he gave up big game hunting in 1970. Even so, he doesn't have anything against those who hunt to eat, but he feels that wild game is a poor substitute for domestically-raised meat. "If chicken, beef and pork weren't the preferred table fare, then why did mankind domesticate animals in the first place?" Bob said.

Since Bob Loveless doesn't hunt anymore, it might seem odd that his primary focus as a knife maker is hunting knives. "My experience during the years that I hunted enabled me to know how to make a knife for big game field care. You don't need a big knife to field dress a deer, antelope or even an elk. A blade in the 3-1/2 to 4-1/2-inch range is more than adequate for the job. Furthermore, a knife has to fit the grip pocket of the hand. If the handle is poorly shaped and difficult to grip, then the knife isn't user-friendly. If a knife maker hasn't spent time in the field and gotten bloody to the elbows, he'll never understand the nature of a hunting knife," Bob said.

Referring to his signature knife, the dropped hunter, Bob said, "Right from the start of my career as a knife maker the dropped hunter was an obvious design. This particular blade pattern gets its name from the way the blade point drops away from the back edge of the knife. This positions the point of blade properly for skinning, as well as providing enhanced strength to the tip."

Due to customer demand, Bob has made a few clip-point blade pattern knives. However, the clip-point doesn't have nearly as much point support as the drop-point and is more easily broken should the user exercise lateral pressure on the blade.

In addition to designing and building knives, out of necessity Bob also became a sheath maker. "The sheath is the house where the knife lives. There are lots of production knives, as well as many bench made knives that have poorly designed and cheaply made sheaths. The sheath reflects the quality of the knife that resides therein. If you see a house and the paint is cracked and peeling, the yard badly overgrown and not maintained, then you know that the resident of that house takes little pride in that home. Likewise, a knife maker that doesn't house his knives in a quality sheath reflects on the quality of both the craftsmanship and materials in the knife therein," Bob said.

The Loveless sheath is hand-crafted from 8-9-ounce, top grade cow hide. Every sheath is made to fit snugly so the knife won't accidentally be released from containment. Interestingly, Bob abhors keeper straps. "If they're not sewn or riveted directly to the sheath, the damn things are easily lost. If a rivet is used, then it can scratch the heck out of the knife handle. Should you get entangled in some heavy brush while hunting; even the best snap system can come loose in the field. And there goes your knife," Bob said.

As the first decade of the 21st Century comes to a

The dropped hunter, shown here with a beautiful wood handle and brass single guard, is the design most associated with Loveless' work.

R.W. LOVELESS
maker.
Riverside. Calif.

close, you'll find Bob Loveless living in the same house that he moved into nearly 40 years ago. While knife production has fallen to as few as 30 to 40 knives annually in recent years, Bob still remains actively involved in the business. "I've been retired for some time, but I still do all of the designing and help out in the actual work wherever I am able," Bob said.

Even to an occasional visitor, it's obvious that Bob's shop is where he's truly at home. Everything he needs, from a cup of coffee to music, movies and books, can all be found within arm's reach. His desk is often littered with an eclectic assortment of items that he has either acquired or made over the years.

When asked to sum up his life's work, Bob simply stated, "Do better, and help others." Most certainly he has accomplished all of that and more. His design influence can be seen in nearly every line of production hunting knives. Likewise, most of the knife makers that have come along behind him have freely copied his designs in their own work. There is no doubt his knives will stand as a tribute to his life for generations to come.

In his work shop is where Bob Loveless is really at home. He is shown here in the shop grinding room with more abrasive belts than most knife makers ever use. (Image: Durwood Hollis)

SCHRADE
U.S.A.
· LOVELESS ·

SCHRADE U.S.A.

R.W. LOVELESS ▶
maker
◀ Lawndale, California

[PHOTOS BY HIRO SOGA]

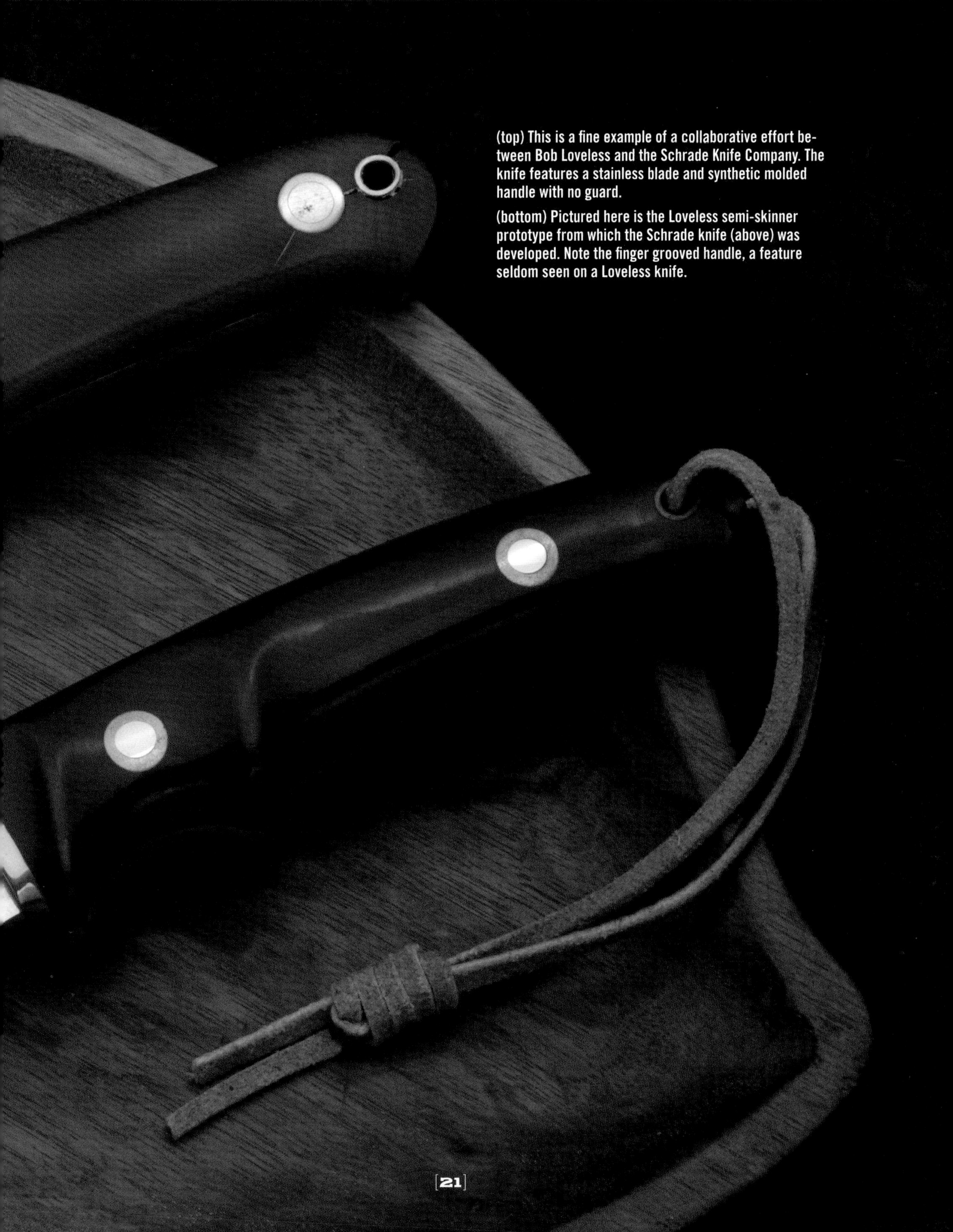

(top) This is a fine example of a collaborative effort between Bob Loveless and the Schrade Knife Company. The knife features a stainless blade and synthetic molded handle with no guard.

(bottom) Pictured here is the Loveless semi-skinner prototype from which the Schrade knife (above) was developed. Note the finger grooved handle, a feature seldom seen on a Loveless knife.

This stag-handled Mini Wilderness knife was made when Loveless resided in Lawndale, California. The knife has a clip-point stainless blade and a double guard.

This all-metal (which allows for sterilization) Loveless surgeon's knife features a drop-point blade design. Only two of these knives were ever made.

R.W. LOVELESS ▷
maker
Lawndale, California ▷

◁ R.W. LOVELESS ▷
maker
▷ Riverside, Calif. ▷

Loveless created this knife for carving
small pieces of wood. The abrupt drop-point
blade is just 2-1/2" in length, and the collar
between the blade and the wood handle
features some fine engraving.

CHAPTER TWO

Words of Wisdom
FROM BOB LOVELESS

BOB LOVELESS SHARES HIS VIEWS ON KNIVES, KNIFE DESIGN AND THE MATERIALS THAT MAKE HIS KNIVES SO VERY SPECIAL

Over the course of several months, author Hollis conducted a series of candid interviews with Bob Loveless about a wide range of knife making subjects.

Hollis: What was it that made you believe that making a knife was possible?

Loveless: "Today (2009) people think that they're going through a difficult financial period. When I came up during the Great Depression, those were really tough times. Fortunately, I lived on my grandparents farm and there was always enough to eat. When it came to other things, there was no extra money to purchase everything that kids today take for granted. If I wanted something, then it had to be made, usually by my own hands.

"Later on, during the course of my duty in the Merchant Marine, a lot of time was spent making repairs and building new parts. I never had any doubt that a knife was beyond my ability. After all, a knife is an extremely simple tool, with limited component parts. Right from the start, I never doubted my ability to make a good knife."

Hollis: In the beginning, did you ever have an idea that would eventually become a knife maker?

Loveless: "Not really. Happenstance pushed me in that direction. What I want in a knife wasn't available and a snippy salesman at Abercrombie & Fitch in New York City set the whole thing in motion. When I discovered that others wanted to buy knives, the stage was set."

(opposite) The author spent several hours interviewing Bob Loveless in his Riverside, California, workshop. The answers that were provided to the many questions that were posed offer insight to a wide range of knife-related subjects. (Image: Hiro Soga)

Hollis: "You indicated that the first knives you built were forged from round stock. What made you switch from forging to stock removal?"

Loveless: "I had no idea that flat stock in the steel of my choice (Jessop 139B nickel-alloy) was available. When I ran out of steel, I contacted the manufacturer. The woman who

An early Loveless knife combines a handle crafted from leather washers with a brass single guard and an aluminum butt-cap. (Image: John Denton)

answered the telephone suggested that I try their flat stock. I realized right then and there that I'd forged my last knife. Her suggestion was what you might call 'a light bulb moment.' When that light came on in my head, I realized that there was no point in beating a piece of round steel stock flat, when you can buy it flat already. No matter what the forging community believes, you can't improve a piece of steel by heating and beating on it."

Hollis: What did your first knives look like?

Loveless: "Basically, they looked a lot like knives that Bo Randall produced. The knives all had narrow tangs, single guards, leather washer handles with finger grooves and an aluminum pommel. Looking back, there is really no comparison between what we produce now and those early knives. They might have been good, solid edged tools, but they were lacking in esthetics. Thankfully, over the years I've been able to break out of that early mold and create knives that not only are functional, but also look good."

Hollis: Some makers continue to put finger grooves in their knife handles. Is that an advantage, or not?

Loveless: "Early on, I made leather washer handles with four finger grooves. I thought at the time that the grooves would provide the user with a better hand-to-knife handle contact. When a knife is used in field-dressing or skinning, all of the initial cuts are made with the cutting edge positioned upward. This means that the knife is actually held upside-down. In that position, finger grooves serve no purpose and actually get in the way of a secure grip. That was the end of finger grooved handles on my knives."

Hollis: What steels are you primarily using now?

Loveless: "We use ATS-34 and BG-42. Most Loveless knife customers seem to be happy with the performance of ATS-34. If you're going to use one of our knives for a lot of field-dressing, skinning and other field care activities, then we suggest using BG-42. That particular steel provides about 10% more edge retention over ATS-34. That said, BG-42 also demands about 10% more effort to make the blades."

Hollis: Do you do your own heat treating?

Loveless: "The very first knife made back in 1953 was heated over a galley stove aboard the ship where I was working at the time. After heating, the blade was quenched in refrigerate oil. When the edge of that knife started to manifest

This close-up image clearly shows the initials "R. W. L," an early Loveless logo. Note the abrasive marks still left in the blade, something you won't find on the mirror-polished blades produced in the current Riverside, California, shop. (Image: John Denton)

This dropped hunter, with its beautiful stag handle, stainless steel single guard and pins, is a product of the Loveless Riverside shop. You'll also note that the "R. W. Loveless" signature appears in the logo. (Image: John Denton)

problems, it was suggested that the blade might be a bit too hard.

"After reading up on heat-treatment at a local library, I learned about tempering. I went back to the ship, stripped the guard and handle off of the blade and used low heat to take draw some of the hardness out of the blade. After that, the knife worked just fine, without any edge problem. Today, I send my knife blanks to Paul Bos for heat-treatment. He's absolutely the best at what he does."

Hollis: Why the big shift away from carbon steel to stainless steel blades?

Loveless: "In a word: laziness. When I was child during the Great Depression, we didn't have much of anything. What we had, we took care of. That meant vehicles, farm equipment, firearms and knives. Today, nobody seems to take care of anything. We have become a disposable society. 'Use it, abuse it and then get a new one' is the current approach to everything.

"When a knife is put to work, afterwards is should be cleaned free of contaminants. If you don't clean a carbon steel knife right away, it's going to stain and rust. Even though a stainless steel blade will eventually rust, a fact learned firsthand by those who thought stainless meant 'no rust ever.' It takes far less care than a comparable carbon steel knife. And that's the primary reason carbon steel knives have fallen out of favor."

Hollis: Stainless steel seems to get a mixed reception when it comes to edge holding and sharpening. To what do you attribute this?

Loveless: "Fifty years ago, carbon steel knives were quite popular. They provided acceptable edge retention and were quite easy to sharpen. In the later part of the last century and into the new millennium, stainless steel knives emerged as the blade steel of choice. The stainless blade alloys are far more complex than those found in carbon steel and offered an outstanding combination of superior edge holding and relative ease of sharpening,

particularly with the more recently developed sharpening technology.

"Some still hold to the belief that carbon steel knives hold their edge longer and are easier to sharpen than stainless. The truth of the matter is that edge holding and sharpening ease are at opposite ends of the spectrum. A knife cannot possess both characteristics at the same time. If a blade is easy to sharpen, then it will not retain that edge for an extended period of time. Conversely, if particular blade steel offers enhanced edge retention, then it will be difficult to sharpen once the edge has become degraded."

Hollis: What led to the dropped (drop-point) hunter blade concept?

Loveless: "It just made sense. When an animal is field-dressed, a hunter must open the abdominal cavity. Unless you're very careful, a clip- or trailing-point blade can easily slice into the underlying viscera. When that happens, you end up with stomach contents, including caustic digestive fluids, all over the inside of the animal.

"Unlike both the clip- and the trailing-point blade patterns, which are crated by taking a concave 'clip' out of the back of the blade, the dropped hunter uses a convex curve to shift the position of the blade tip down and away from the direct line of the back of the blade. Configured in this manner, when you're field-dressing the tip of the blade is less likely to come into contact with the abdominal contents. The same thing is true when skinning. The dropped blade tip is positioned away from the muscle tissue beneath the hide."

Hollis: When you first began making knives, a blade feature called a 'blood groove' was popular on fixed-blade knives. What was that all about?

Loveless: "The so-called 'blood groove' or fuller was supposed to allow blood to flow freely from the animal once the blade was inserted. Farm animals are usually stunned first, before being slaughtered. Since the animal is still alive, the heart continues to pump blood. When the arteries in the neck are cut, the blood in the circulatory system is simply pumped out. At that time, many hunters either had a rural background or were taught field care by their fathers who came from the farm. They thought that whatever was done on the farm also extended to wild game in the field.

"The truth of the matter is that in an animal taken with a firearm or archery gear, it is dead and the heart no longer functions. As a result of bullet or arrow penetration, all of the blood tends to pool inside the animal. The bottom line is that a 'blood groove' on a knife blade really doesn't serve its intended purpose, other than purely decorative. Hunters must have learned this, because this feature isn't found on many blades today."

When talking about some of the logos that have appeared on his knives through the years, Loveless broke into a broad smile when asked about his "Naked Lady" logo. "She's still around," Loveless said. (Image: Hiro Soga)

Hollis: What do you believe is the ideal blade length for a hunting knife?

Loveless: "A blade 3-1/2 inches long is just about right for big game field work. You can keep your index finger along the back of the blade and know the position of the cutting edge at all times, even when working blind inside of the chest cavity of an animal. Longer blades can be usable, but the added length tends to make the knife a bit unwieldy. A shorter blade tends to draw you into the work, making things more difficult than necessary."

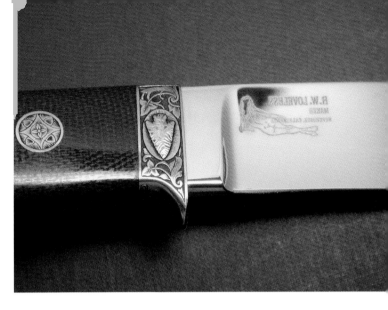

Hollis: Some makers accessorized their hunting knives with file work on the back of the blade. Is this a useful feature, or not?

Loveless: "A Loveless knife is everything a knife should be. Adding additional features won't improve performance. File work on the back of a blade is often more decorative than functional. Some of the file work I've seen, now called 'jimping' by some, is so rough that it's uncomfortable. If a knife fits the hand properly, then all the control you need is accomplished by the handle, not a thumb or forefinger bearing down on the blade back."

Hollis: I constantly encounter makers who believe that a convex-ground cutting edge provides the best performance. What do think?

Loveless: "Nearly everyone has a tough time sharpening a knife. That being the case, what do you think happens to a convex edge when it needs to be sharpened? Even with the best edge restoration tools, what was once convex will quickly become a flat, tapered edge. A convex edge sounds good in advertising literature, but in reality it's very difficult for the user to replicate that geometry when the need arises."

This rather ornate piece has both the "Riverside, California" blade mark and the famous Loveless "Naked Lady." (Image: John Denton)

Hollis: Over the years you've used many different blade marks, including the famous naked lady. Can you tell us about how your blade marks evolved?

Loveless: "My first blade mark was simply "Delaware Maid." I don't recall what it was that gave rise to that mark, but I was living in the state of Delaware at that time. Some of those knives even had "R. W. Loveless, Maker, Claymont Del." included in the logo. Since the Abercrombie & Fitch sporting goods store in New York City were the ones who first ordered knives, their name was also placed on the obverse side of the blade.

A few of those early knives even had the words "Loveless Made" rather than "Delaware Maid." Rather than being etched, as is currently done in my Riverside shop, all of those early knives were marked with a vibrator-type marking tool by hand. The "Delaware Maid" mark lasted until the late 1950s. Shortly after I came to California in 1959 I dropped the "Delaware Maid" mark and just used "R. W. Loveless Maker." When we settled in Lawndale, California, I used "R. W. Loveless –maker –Lawndale, California."

"In the early 1960s, I learned about chemical etching and that has been my usual method of blade marking ever since. The first few knives that had etched marks were marked "Loveless and Parke Makers - Sierra Madre, California." Bill Parke was an investor in my knife making business. He put up the funds and I made the knives, probably about four dozen knives. That association didn't last too long. When we dissolved our limited partnership, his name was dropped from the logo. Afterwards, I returned to using "R. W. Loveless – Maker – Lawndale, California."

"As I recall, in the late 1960s and early 1970s, Barry Wood was a knife maker who lived in the Venice, California, area. He had designed a unique folding knife, and he and I collaborated on a few folders. The blade mark on those knives was "Wood/Loveless – makers – Venice, California."

(right) This unusual knife bears the "Lawndale, California" blade mark. Note the cracks in the ivory handle. This is the reason, Loveless believes, that natural ivory is a very poor knife handle material. You can get the same look with white Micarta without any possibility of yellowing with age or cracking. (Image: John Denton)

(below) This knife bears the "Loveless & Johnson" blade mark and was produced in the early 1970s when Steve Johnson worked with Bob Loveless. Johnson now resides in Utah and is a prominent knife maker whose knives manifest a strong Loveless influence. (Image: John Denton)

(opposite) These two stag-handled beauties both have the "Naked Lady" blade mark. The top knife has a narrow guard and double pins, which are made out of stainless steel. The bottom knife has a much broader stainless guard and there are no handle pins. (Image: John Denton)

"When Steve Johnson came to work with me in the early 1970s, I introduced a new logo, "Loveless & Johnson – makers – Riverside, California." Of course, I'd moved to Riverside, where my home and shop are now located. Also, I made a few knives in Riverside that had the old "Delaware Maid" logo included with my usual mark. Those knives were commemoratives and featured stacked leather washer handles and an aluminum butt cap.

"In 1976, at the Guild Show, in addition to my usual logo, I introduced the famous "Naked Lady" etched on the blade just below my mark. You see her front side in repose on the logo side of the knife. Turn the blade over and you see the reverse. She appeared on my knives for a number of years. Political correctness being what it is, she is a little shy these days. However, she's still around.

"When Jim

Merritt came to work in the shop, the "Loveless – Merritt – makers – Riverside, California" made its appearance for a short time. A couple of other marks, including one with my signature, also were used. For many years now, I've simply used "R. W. Loveless – maker – Riverside, California."

Hollis: You seem to favor blade guards in your work. What's the advantage?

Loveless: "A guard protects the knife user from accidentally having their forefinger slip forward off of the handle and onto the blade. Should that happen, there could be serious consequences. A double guard, often found in a fighting knife, does the same thing and also allows the user to parry a knife attack. The attacker's blade will slide along the tope of the defender's knife blade and be stopped by the top portion of the guard."

Hollis: The tapered blade tang is another feature found on your later knives. What brought that about?

Loveless: "Before the tangs on my blades were tapered, the knives we made always seemed a bit handle heavy. Just a couple of years into knife making, a friend gave me an old Lamson and Goodnow knife that had a fully tapered tang. What was interesting about that knife was the design dated back to the mid-1800s. Later on, when attempting to salvage some blades that had warped during heat-treatment, I decided to taper the tangs as a method of restoring straightness to the blade blank. After straightening the blank and assembling the knives, I realized that the tapered tang was the way to go. Not only had the tapering saved a number of warped blanks, but it also changed the knife balance, moving it forward to the mid-point of the knife near the guard. Some makers drill holes in their tangs to accomplish the same thing. I just think a tapered tang gives a knife that very special look"

Hollis: The use of red fiber spacers with green canvas Micarta handle material seems to be a Loveless trademark. Any reason why?

Loveless: "I like a little color on a knife. A touch of the right shade of lipstick can improve a woman's looks. Likewise, a red fiber spacer imparts a special something to my knives. Micarta handle material is a favorite because it's nearly indestructible. Even if you get a scratch on it, it's an easy matter to buff it right out. And I like green canvas Micarta because the color and the canvas

pattern seem to fit well in most hunting venues."

Hollis: You've built some really nice stag handled knives. Does that mean stag is the best handle material for a hunting knife?

Loveless: "Over the years, I've used stag on both full-tang and narrow-tang knives. It used to be my favorite handle material until customers starting returning knives that had chipped and cracked handles. Drop a stag handled knife on a hard surface and it's apt to suffer damage. Also, improperly aged stag can crack over time. In both instances, the only solution is handle replacement and that can be costly. Really good stag has gotten harder and harder to get these days. When you find a source, the cost can be prohibitive. Axis deer and European red stag can work as a substitute, but neither one possesses the quality of true Indian Sambar stag."

Hollis: What are some of the other handle materials you've worked with?

Loveless: "I've used desert ironwood extensively. It doesn't need to be stabilized to prevent cracking and the figure in the grain imparts a warm and vibrant look. While many other tropical hardwoods are also naturally very stable, they tend to have a dark and brooding appearance. The same thing is true about the near monotone look of buffalo horn. Unless horn has been stabilized, a step many makers don't think is important,

The "Bird's Head" look to the handle terminus of this Loveless stag-handled knife not only imparts a distinctive look, but it also serves to help lock the hand to the handle. The R. W. Loveless signature on the sheath also sets his work apart from other makers. (Image: John Denton)

(below) It was obvious during the author's many discussions with Bob Loveless that his workshop is where he's truly at home. (Image: Hiro Soga)

horn has a tendency to shrink and crack over time. And horn will chip and crack if dropped on a hard surface. In my opinion, Micarta is the ultimate handle material. It isn't affected by oil, water and most chemicals. It can take a lot of hard knocks without chipping or cracking and minor damage can easily be repaired."

Hollis: Tell me about the design characteristics of a Loveless fixed-blade knife handle.

Loveless: "My knife handles are made to fit the hand, no matter what size. A slender, elliptical handle design fits everyone, no mater whether your hand is small or large. And that's just the kind of grip you'll find on one of my knives.

"Our military discovered this same fact when they contracted for the Colt Model 1911, .45 caliber pistol. The handle on that pistol is relatively slender, with slighty rounded grips. Because it's not too big, anyone can grip it easily. The Beretta pistol in use now has a much thicker grip, due to the increased clip capacity, and is far more difficult to grasp securely when you have smaller hands."

Hollis: What's the purpose of the bird's head look at the end of your knife handles?

Loveless: "What you call a 'bird's head' actually helps keep the knife securely positioned in the hand. It's a design feature that gives knife handles viable ergonomics, as well as a distinctive 'Loveless' look."

Hollis: Collaborations with many domestic makers have spawned a whole new era of off-shore produced and very affordable production handmade knife clones. Has this had an impact on your business?

Loveless: "Not really. There is still far more demand for one of my knives made right here in Riverside than both my business partner and I have the time and energy to build. I've designed knives in collaboration with other cutlery firms; Gerber, Schrade, Beretta and Lone Wolf come to mind. The work was primarily so that the average guy can own a Loveless-designed knife at an affordable price. That's a 'win, win' for both the customer and myself."

Hollis: At knife shows we see many knives that are highly ornate and fit into the 'art knife' category. Do you see any of your work fitting into that market?

Loveless: "Most of the knives I've made were designed to be working tools. Nothing gives me more satisfaction than when a customer calls or writes and tells me how well one of my knives performed in the field. Of course, a few of my knives have been engraved and sold for exorbitant sums, but that wasn't my original intent. I just want to make the best knife possible."

Hollis: What do you think are the most significant changes in the cutlery industry since you first began making knives?

Loveless: "When I built my first knife, there were only a handful of makers in the country. Rudy Ruana, Bill Moran and Bo Randall are the ones that come to mind. Even though it wasn't hard to make a knife in those days, making a living as a knife maker was hard to do. Obviously, building knives wasn't high on the list of popular professions 50 years ago. Even now, most knife makers struggle to make a living.

"One of the most obvious changes in the cutlery industry is that proliferation of those who are actively involved in building handmade knives, here in the U. S., as well as Europe and Japan. Every year, more and more handmade knife makers are seen at knife shows and advertising in knife magazines. Given the fact that you can purchase a good knife from almost any of the production cutlery factories, I'd of never thought the public would be that interested in handmade knives.

"Another huge change is cutlery diversity. In addition to traditional knife designs for everyday use, fishing and hunting, now we also have tactical knives, art knives, diving knives, knife contained multi-tools and a host of other cutlery categories that were non-existent 50 years ago.

"Of course, the change from fixed-blade knives to folders, particularly lock-blade folding designs, has had a dynamic impact on the cutlery industry. Currently, only about 20% of the knives sold are fixed-blade models. That's a huge difference from the mid-point of the last century. Back then, if you were a big game hunter, you carried a fixed-blade knife. Now, just the opposite is true.

"Just as significant is the loss of several well-respected production knife companies. Schrade, Camillus, Western and several others are now no longer in business. While the trademarks have been purchased by others, the original plants have all been closed. Gone also are a great number of veteran cutlery makers who worked within those operations. Labor in this country is so costly that much of the work has been shifted to offshore manufacturers. Sadly, America is losing its cutlery roots."

Both of these Loveless knives feature engraving. The top knife has only a touch on the guard, while the bottom knife has far more elaborate work encompassing both the guard and the pins in the handle. (Image: John Denton)

Hollis: You've said earlier that the demand for your knives far exceeds the production capability. Are you taking orders? If not, how can someone acquire a Loveless knife?

Loveless: "I've been retired from active involvement in knife making for a number of years. I do continue to make minor adjustments on many of my designs and Jim Merritt still builds Loveless knives here in the shop. He's a full-partner in the business and an outstanding knife maker. I still get involved with the work when I can, but Jim is the main one building knives right now.

"I haven't accepted any new knife orders for quite some time. The few knives we build here in the shop usually go directly to a couple of prominent dealers. John Denton (jwdenton@windstream.net) probably handles more of my knives annually than any other dealer. If you're serious about acquiring one of my knives, that's the place to start."

Hollis: Any parting words for those wanting to learn to build knives?

Loveless: "You'll never know whether or not you can accomplish a task until you try. Many never take the first step. You have to know within yourself that you can do it. If you can work a wrench, use a screwdriver or hammer a nail, you can make a knife. It's easy to make knife, but difficult to make a living at it.

"My goal has always been to produce the very best knife possible. Looking over my body of work, I see a lot of mistakes. The good thing about knife making is you can always correct a mistake with the next knife. If I could sum it all up, I'd say do better each time and pass it on."

While horn can shrink and crack over time, it still makes for a lovely knife handle. The Loveless dropped hunter, made in the Riverside, California, shop, clearly demonstrates that fact.

Made in 1973, when Steve Johnson worked with Bob Loveless, this drop-point hunter features hidden tang construction, a single guard and a maroon Micarta handle.

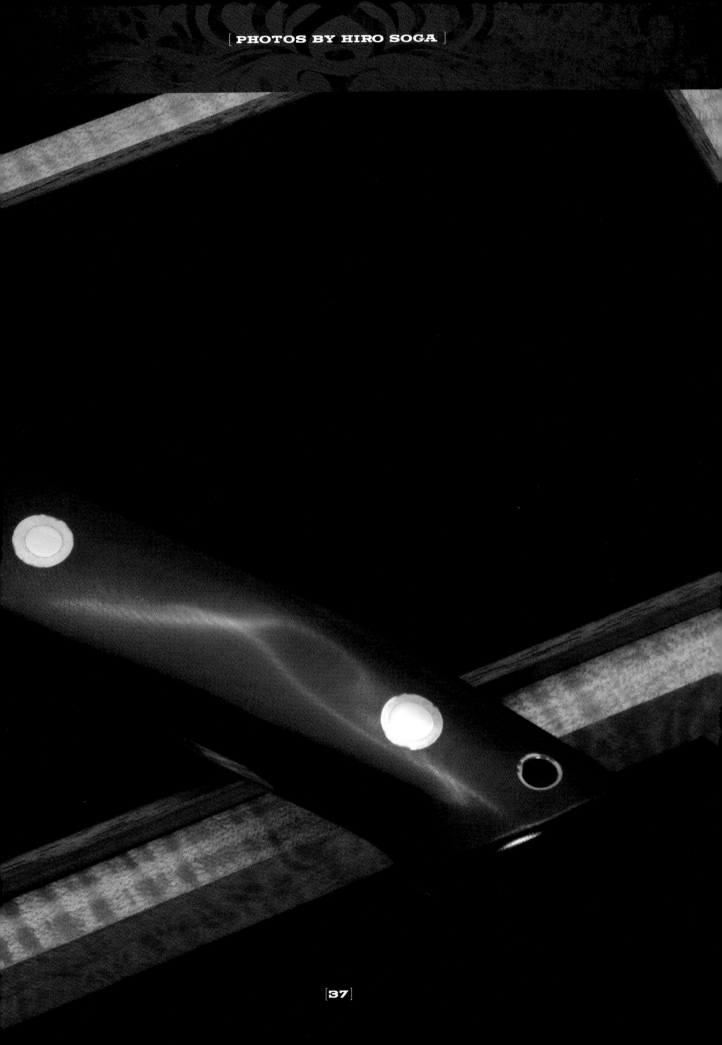

One of the most rare (only 36 were ever marked
with the "Loveless-Parke" logo) and sought-after
knives ever made by Loveless, this kitchen/camp
knife was made in 1967. The knife features an
ivory improved handle and hidden tang.

R.W. LOVELESS
maker
Riverside, Calif.

Loveless said that this integral semi-skinner, with its dark green canvas Micarta handle, is "the most beautiful knife I ever made." The knife was crafted about 1987 and features a drop-point blade pattern.

This crown stag (two-piece handle) utility
knife was produced by Loveless about 1978.
The blade features a drop-point pattern
and the reclining nude logo. Loveless once
remarked that "it is quite a special knife."

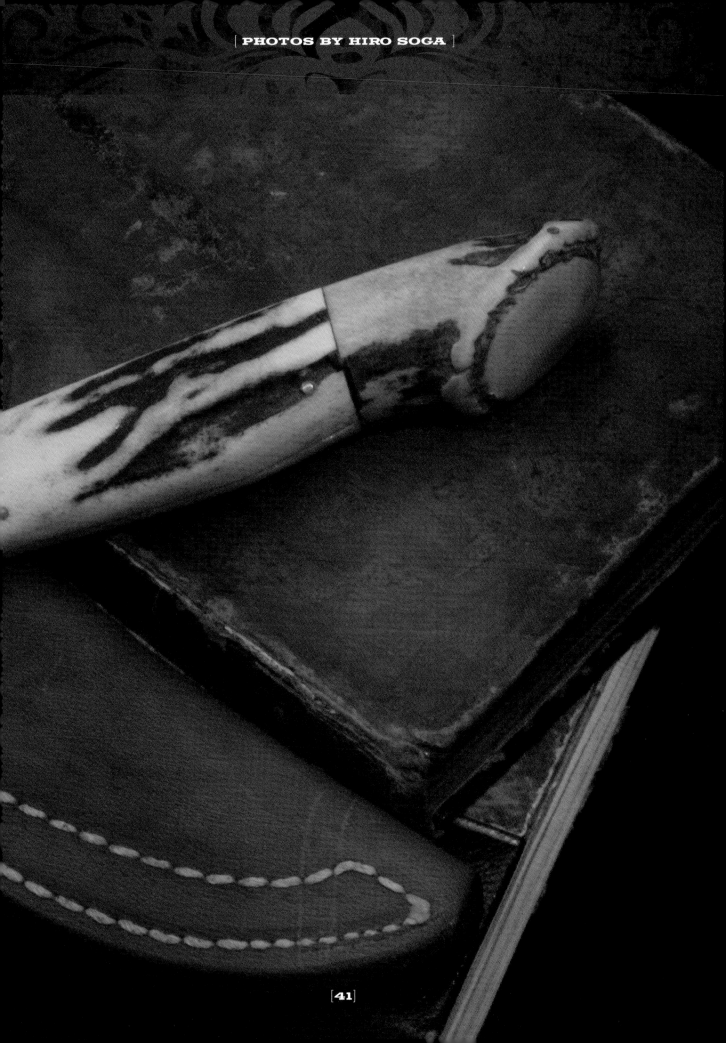

CHAPTER THREE

Tools of the Trade

HIGH~TECH TOOLS ARE NOT NECESSARY: FUNCTIONAL CUTLERY CAN BE MADE EVEN WITH SIMPLE HAND TOOLS

From the outset, man as a distinct species has always been defined as a tool maker. While there are certain apes, particularly chimpanzees, that have been seen using naturally occurring objects as tools, that use doesn't include any high degree of object modification. It's a far cry from a chimp wetting a piece of grass with saliva and using it to extract termites from a mound, to even the earliest species of man making and using stone tools.

At some point in man's prehistory, he learned to modify objects found in his environment to enhance hunting and food gathering. Hardening the point of a stick in the hot coals of a fire produced a far more effective spear. Likewise, bones were abraded and rocks chipped until a cutting edge was produced.

It also became apparent to man that object modification required the use of something capable of that activity, meaning that another type of tool was a necessity. Since weapons and tools often had to be made on the spot, man carried his tool-making supplies with him. It's easy to imagine how all of this evolved from a few simple tools carried by hand, to a tool pouch, to a tool box, to a garage shop and finally to a larger manufacturing facility.

Today, a hobbyist knife maker may set up shop in a spare room in an apartment or home, using nothing more than an assortment of hand tools. With a knife kit, available from most knife supply outlets, he becomes a knife maker. In some instances, because knife making can be dirty and noisy, the novice knife maker may locate his work area in a garage. And the experienced knife maker may have a separate shop entirely

(opposite) The very first tools in your shop should be pen and paper. Here, Bob Loveless is shown at his desk making notes on a new knife design. (Image: Durwood Hollis)

devoted to these activities. In every instance, however, the use of tools will be a necessary component of knife manufacture.

Should you ever have an occasion to enter into a knife maker's shop, you will be struck with the large number of tools found therein. More than one individual who had the desire to make their own knife has had that desire quenched at the outset by just such an experience.

According to Bob Loveless, "The beginning knife maker can do everything that needs to be done with these tools: a vise, a grinder and an assortment of files (round, half-round and flat) and a pair of safety glasses." Bob went on to say, "It's not hard to make knives, but it's hard to make a living making knives."

Master Blade Smith Wayne Goddard, in his book *$50 Knife Shop: Get Started without Spending a Fortune* (Krause Publications, revised 2006), echoes this opinion. Wayne said, "I could make both forged and stock-

Produced by Krause Publications and written by Master Blade Smith Wayne Goddard, the $50 Knife Shop soft-cover book is filled with solid tool acquisition advice. (Image: Durwood Hollis)

removal projects" with a tool expense of no more than for $50. When Wayne was done buying his basic tools, he had $14 left. Adding $2 to that amount, he built a belt grinder from yard sale parts. For those with meager funds to devote to their budding desire to make knives, especially forging, Wayne's book ought to be required reading.

Loveless went on to say, "The ideal knife shop should contain various hand tools, three different sizes of wheel and belt grinders, six to eight grades of abrasives, a drill press, a small mill and a band saw." Even though brand new tools are great, you can find some fantastic bargains in used tools. Put some calories in haunting Goodwill, surplus stores, Deseret Industries and other used goods outlets. Likewise, yard sales and swap meets are a great source of used hand and machine tools. Furthermore, advertisers in local newspapers may reveal hidden tool treasures that can be had for little outlay of funds.

The work location

When Loveless first started building knives, he set up shop in his basement. "The basement seemed to be the logical location for a shop. It was out of the way of the usual household activities and kept the sound level to a minimum. Most importantly, my wife didn't object to having a workshop in the basement," Bob said. When he lived in Lawndale, California, Loveless operated his knife making business out of a garage. However, the primary reason that he purchased his home in Riverside was the fact that the property had a detached workshop that was separate from the main residence.

The work bench

Bob Loveless has a definite opinion about a knife maker's work bench. "You can purchase a ready-made work bench at many big box stores (Costco, Sam's Club, etc.), or you can make your own. I'd suggest that you make your own to fit wherever you do your work. All it takes is about a dozen 2x4s and a few 6x6s. Make the basic frame out of the 6x6s. Rather than laying the 2x4s flat, turn them on-edge and glue and bolt them through and through. Counter-sink the nuts so they won't get in your way. Make sure that the 6x6 support legs are positioned every two feet, so the bench will be adequately supported. You really can't make a knife maker's work bench too heavy. When you're finished building the bench, it should be sturdy enough that a hammer won't bounce when the bench is hit. A piece of 1/4 or 3/8-inch plywood, Masonite, or sheet nylon of the same thickness can be used as a bench topper."

Safety gear

The first thing that must always be considered when building knives is safety. Every time you enter your shop to work, wearing protective eyeglasses should be part of the start-up ritual. Likewise, hearing protection is a good idea when

While you can purchase a ready-made work bench, it may not suit your knife building needs. Bob Loveless is shown at the bench he made. "When you're finished building the bench, it should be sturdy enough that a hammer won't bounce when the bench is hit," Bob said. (Image: Durwood Hollis)

forging or working around power equipment. A heavy-duty apron (most experienced makers wear leather aprons) that allows freedom of movement will protect your clothing and person from sparks, spills and other gunk commonly encountered in the work environment. If you plan to do any forging or heat-treating, protective gloves will be an essential part of your knife building wardrobe. Also, it's a good idea to wear comfortable, steel toe footwear in the shop. You never know when a heavy or sharp object will come your way. And long-haired makers should wear a cap to keep their hair out of the way. There's nothing like having your curly locks caught in grinder or buffer. To be safe, think safe.

Tool safety

If you've never hit your thumb with a hammer, then you're among all people most fortunate. Indeed, even hand tools have a certain safety threshold that when crossed can put your person in jeopardy. Add power to any tool and the safety threshold is more like a door opening into a set of stairs. Make a mistake and you can easily tumble down the stairs if don't hold onto the hand rail.

"When possible, work with a partner. If you become injured while working, help is always within voice range. Even with a phone in your work area or a cell phone in your pocket, you may not be able to reach it or manipulate the keys. Working alone in a basement or detached work area puts you in a situation where your shouts for help might not be heard. In such a case, it may be hours before someone comes to your aid," Loveless said.

I am amazed at just how often even known knife makers are pictured working without adequate safety gear. In a recent issue of a popular knife magazine, a maker is shown working at a bandsaw wearing shorts and what appear to be comfortable walking shoes. I believe he was wearing glasses, but they didn't appear to be of the safety variety. When you take a casual approach to working with power tools and steel, then you're far more likely to injure yourself accidentally. At the very least, the individual mentioned above should have been wearing wrap-around safety glasses, full-length pants, steel toe shoes and even a protective apron. Things happen and when they do you can expect the worst outcome. "Think safety every time you step into your work area," Bob Loveless said.

Hammers

Every knife maker needs a selection of hammers. In the Loveless shop you'll find an assortment of ball-peen hammers, ranging in weight from eight ounces to

36 ounces. "I probably use the smaller ones more often than the bigger ones, but at some point every

Every knife maker will need at least one ball-peen hammer. As you can see, there are several in the Loveless workshop. (Image: Durwood Hollis)

hammer in the shop has come in handy. Mostly, a hammer is used to peen pins for handle scale and bolster attachment. However, there are times that a hammer is needed to seat a guard properly," Bob said.

Files

Not everything on a knife can be finished with a belt grinder. For those times, you'll need an assortment of

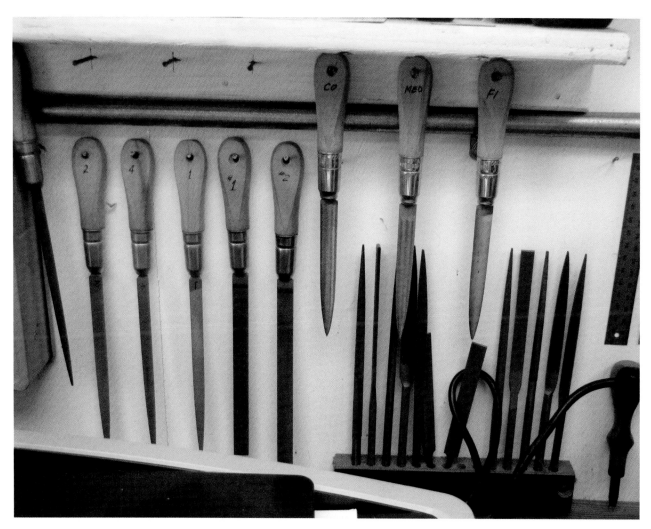

(above) Whether you own a belt grinder or not, knife building will require lots of file work. As you can see, the Loveless shop has a wide assortment of files. (Image: Durwood Hollis)

(left) When it comes to files, you can never have too many. In addition to flat files, Loveless also has several different triangular and round files, in a variety of lengths and diameters. (Image: Durwood Hollis)

files, including flat, half-round, crossing, triangular and rat-tail files. Loveless had "blinded," or ground down smooth the teeth on one side of all of his triangular files. This allows him to work in tight, without worry about accidentally damaging material on the opposite side of the file.

"It's important to keep all of your files clean. You'll need a file card or a wire brush to remove the filings from the teeth. Filings can get work-welded to the file teeth. If they're not removed after every file usage, you'll quickly have a useless tool. While you're at it, keep your files well oiled with extreme pressure oil and you won't have any problem with the files gumming up with filings or rusting," Bob said.

(left) The anvil is the centerpiece of any knife maker's shop. The Loveless anvil came from a railroad maintenance yard and was made from a piece of track. (Image: Durwood Hollis)

(below) While you can purchase a new belt grinder, it's entirely possible to make your own and save some serious money. (Image: Durwood Hollis)

Anvil

Every knife maker needs an anvil. It serves as a rigid surface upon which retaining pins, bolsters and pommels can be set. And you'll find that once the anvil is properly prepared, it has a host of other uses. "My anvil came from a railroad maintenance yard. It's nothing more than a 12-inch length of railroad track. Before it came into my shop, I took the length of track to a machine shop and had the top, as well as a section of the back, milled flat and square. And one end of the piece of track was rounded off to form a horn. Once all of that was done, I had an adequate anvil," Loveless said.

Junk yards always seem to have lengths of railroad track lying around. For a small outlay of funds you can probably have one of the workmen in the yard use a torch to cut a piece of track into the size you require. You just need to think outside of your usual options and an anvil will manifest itself. My fa-

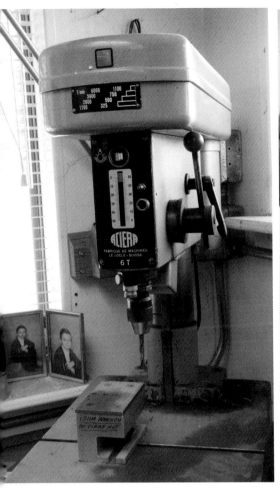

ther purchased an anvil at a farm sale for little more than pocket change. As far as the seller was concerned, the anvil was nothing but scrap metal. What to one is a discard, to another is a treasure in the making.

Grinder

In the Loveless shop you'll see both belt and wheel grinders. "I use a belt grinder far more often than a wheel grinder, but you can run abrasives, wire brushes and buffering wheels all off of one dual axel motor. In reality, both types are important tools to have in your shop," Bob said. You can purchase a new grinder/buffer combination, or build one yourself with easily obtainable components. There are even instructions on building your own grinder/buffer that can be found in books or on the Web that provide step-by-step directions. .

Drill press

A drill press is a knife maker's essential. However, a new drill press can be an expensive proposition. If you're just getting started making knives, an electric hand drill can handle many assignments. In some situations (e.g. drilling a deep hole into handle material for a blind tang), you'll need better support. A drill press fixture, into which the hand drill can be secured, is a better choice than freehand drill use. Once you get into knife making, you'll quickly realize the importance of having a free-standing drill press. While the purchase of a drill press will require an outlay of considerable funds, you will quickly realize the benefit. "My shop has about six drill presses and every one has a use," Loveless said.

ar left) When you're just starting out uilding knives, you may not be able to ford a drill press. However, this is one ece of equipment that can make your e easier. (Image: Durwood Hollis)

ft) In the Loveless shop, there are veral drill presses, each set up for particular job. This way, Bob doesn't ve to waste time changing bits. nage: Durwood Hollis)

elow) It's important to keep your ill press clean and well lubricated. b treats all of his electric-powered ols with the same care as he would y fine tool. (Image: Durwood Hollis)

Drill bits

An assortment of drill bits is necessary, from 1/16 to 1/2 inch, all contained in a case so the bits won't get mixed in with other tools and lost. "Just any drill bit won't do the job. When you purchase drills, select those that are made of Cobalt alloy high-speed steel. Premium drills aren't cheap, but

they won't wear out and ruin your work," Bob said.

Over time, drill bits will break and get damaged in other ways. Typically, the bits that need replacement are those most often used. When you need a replacement, buy two or three of the same size so you don't have to run to the store repeatedly.

Punches

An assortment of various size drift and center punches will come in handy. Drift punches are used to move and set the pins used in handle and bolster attachment. Center punches are used to make an indent in metal prior to drilling a hole. This allows the drill bit to find its natural center point. I like to buy my punches in a set that includes some type of containment. In this way, I don't have to dig through a bunch of tools, just to find a punch. While you're at it, buy a couple of different size center punches. One size might work, but you're better off with a selection.

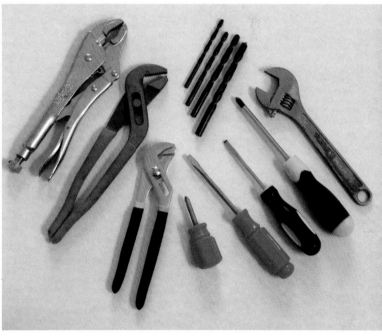

Assorted hand tools

Over time the knife maker will acquire a wide assortment of hand tools, including screwdrivers (flat and Allen head),

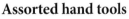
Every knife maker will need an assortment of hand tools and drill bits. You don't have to have brand new gear. Look for used tools at yard sales, thrift shops and junkyards. (Image: Durwood Hollis)

pliers (round and flat jaws, tapered jaws, needle-nose and Vise-grip type), hack saw, coping saw, a square and leather working tools. "While a knife maker will never be finished acquiring tools, the most important ones will be those on your work bench; either mounted to it or laying thereon. Your own work will teach you what you need in tools," Bob said.

Hand tools don't always have to be brand new. You can often find tool bargains at yard sales, second-hand stores and the classified section of your local newspaper. The same thing, however, isn't always true for power equipment. While you can use old working washing machine motors, pulleys, belts and assorted parts salvaged from a junk yard to make electrical powered equipment, it's not the best approach. Power tools and equipment can be dangerous, and the danger level increases exponentially when using something that was junk to begin with.

Forge

When Loveless first started making knives, the only experience he had was what he had learned by spending time with Bo Randall. "I purchased a small forge that had a 6-inch square throat with about 14 inches of depth, and my first dozen or so knives were all forged from 3/4-inch round bar stock. It was the old heat-and-beat routine and it was hard work. When I ran out of my initial supply of steel (Jessop 139B nickel steel), I called Jessop Steel to place an order. The person on the other end of the telephone suggested that rather than heating and beating 3/4-inch round bar stock flat, using their flat stock (1/4x1-inch) would make the work a lot easier.

ply outlets), scribing the knife outline on the steel and then removing everything that's not important. When asked, Bob will tell you that his actions as a maker only "frees" the blade that he has already visualized within the steel.

That said, there are those that, after dabbling in knife making for awhile, want to forge their own blade. There are small, affordable gas-operated blade forges that can be found at most knife supply outlets or direct from the manufacturer. Before you invest in a forge, however, make sure you really are serious about starting down that path. Forging your own blade can be gratifying and enjoyable, but expect an extended learning curve before you become proficient. Forging and stock removal both arrive at the same destination, but do so by following two entirely different paths.

Stay organized

In Bob Loveless' shop, every tool has its own place. Rather than keeping a jumble of tools in several drawers, Bob has most of his hand tools hanging above the various work benches. The tools are aligned in order of both application and size. The same thing is true with the various power tools and their accessories. Everything is kept in an orderly fashion.

"Looking for a tool can be a big time-waster. If your tools are scattered all around the shop, it's difficult to find what want when you need it. When things are well organized, you can go to right to whatever tool the job at hand demands," Bob said.

Knife building mentors

Sadly, knife making apprentice programs are almost a thing of the past in this country. Such programs will teach you what tools to acquire and how to use them. Europe, however, still has an apprentice system to develop qualified journeymen.

According to Loveless, "If you have the time and means, a visit to one or more Continental knife manufacturing operations can be a real eye-opener. You'll see what kind of tools are needed and used on a regular basis."

A trip to Europe just to visit a knife manufacturing operation may be impractical. There are, however, several stateside makers that offer classes. In a class setting you'll learn what tools are needed and how to use them properly. Every dime you spend in a hands-on teaching environment is a solid investment in your future as a knife maker.

Clean and well-maintained

All too often, many of us neglect our tools. They're used and turned-off, or put away without any thought given to cleaning and periodic maintenance. Over time, grease and metal particles can build up and impair proper functioning. This is particular true when it comes to power tools.

Right then and there I had what you might call a light bulb moment. That ended my forging career and was the beginning of what has come to be known as stock removal knife making," Bob said.

I think it's safe to say that many of the knives being made today are produced by the "stock-removal" method. This involves the purchase of appropriately-sized blade stock (this can be obtained from most knife sup-

Every shop should have a supply of clean rags. After you complete a particular job, wipe off the tools that you used prior to returning them to their storage location. Since metal filing can get work-weld to file teeth, use a file card after every use to keep your files in good working order.

Also, you'll find that some grit and grime doesn't clean up easily. This is where compressed air can come to the rescue. Even if you don't have a compressor and an air hose in your shop, you can purchase canned air, which can be found anywhere computers are sold, and use that to blow out metal shaving from hard-to-reach locations.

Any tool that has moving parts needs an occasional shot of oil. There are several types of spray lubricants that can be employed. Keep a can in a convenient location and use it when needed. It's far better to keep your power tools well lubricated than it is to wait until a component seizes up and then shell out cash for a repair or replacement.

Lastly, keep a regular broom, a whisk broom and a dustpan in a location near the entrance to your shop. This way they will be silent reminders to sweep up the shop when the work is done. An old song says, "Turn out the lights, the party's over." Well, make sure you clean up and sweep before "you turn out the lights."

Ventilation

Airborne particles can be problematic. When breathed in, this type of dust can travel deep into your lungs and lodge there permanently. Anything that contains silica, when taken into the body through respiration, can cause scarring and impair lung capacity.

Some types of handle materials are flat-out deadly and their dust should never be inhaled. Likewise, tiny metal particles suspended in the air during grinding don't make for the most maker-friendly interior workshop atmosphere. Wearing a simple protective mask when grinding or buffing is a step in the right direction, but that alone isn't enough. A respirator should be considered in most of these types of work situations. The best approach is a combination of a respirator and some mechanism to vent noxious dust and fumes from your shop.

Noise

Extended periods of continuous noise will wear you out. And some sound levels can cause permanent hearing loss. Even the bang of a hammer seating a rivet can lead to ringing in the ears. Foam ear plugs are inexpensive and will help reduce the level of noise in your shop. However, when you're running a power tool (grinder, buffer, saw, etc.), it's best to use ear muffs for en-

hanced protection. Hearing loss doesn't happen right away, but if you fail to protect your ears that loss is inevitable.

The bottom line

When you're building a knife, pay close attention to what whatever task is at hand. Knife work isn't time for multi-tasking. Keep all potential distractions (kids, pets, etc.), as well as anything (the game of the week on television) or anyone (spouses, friends, etc.) that can distract you, out of the shop when you're working. That same thing applies to alcohol consumption. Even a small amount can impair your judgment. Adult beverages have no place in a knife maker's work shop. Finally, if something outside of the work environment needs immediate attention, stop what you're doing before you attempt to deal with the situation.

"Most knife work is nothing more than hand labor. That's why it's possible to make a knife with nothing but hand tools. It's done all day long in parts of Asia, Latin American and the Middle East," Loveless said.

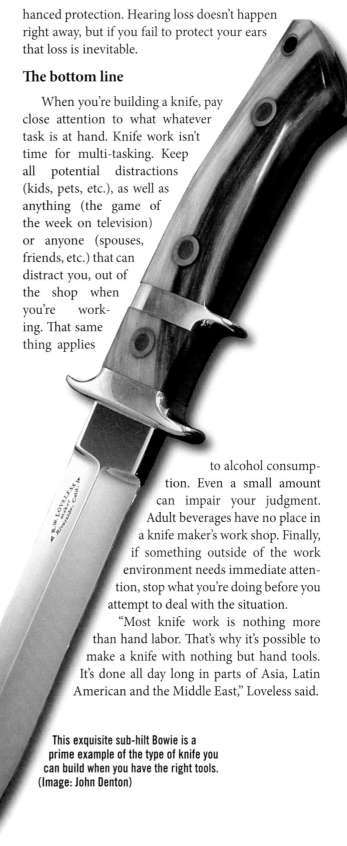

This exquisite sub-hilt Bowie is a prime example of the type of knife you can build when you have the right tools. (Image: John Denton)

R.W. LOVELESS
maker
Riverside, Calif.

Featuring an extra-wide bolster with engraving by
Jon Robyn of Monet's famous "Olympia" painting,
this Loveless knife is a beauty to behold.

This Loveless dropped-hunter is one-third size and
features a 3-1/2" blade, with engraving by Bruce Shaw.

Made on October 12, 1986, this fixed-blade features a slender 4" drop-point blade and the now famous Loveless reclining nude logo.

R.W. LOVELESS
MAKER
RIVERSIDE CALIF

CHAPTER FOUR

Blade Work

TAKING A PIECE OF STEEL STOCK TO A READY-FOR-HANDLE BLADE IS BOTH CHALLENGING AND REWARDING

Building a knife is a process. This chapter outlines the steps involved in taking a piece of flat steel stock and creating a ready-for-handle blade. Before you start, however, realize that knife making isn't something that happens in a hurry. Patience and a continuing commitment to safety are both essential qualities of any craftsman. If you rush the work, untoward events are bound to occur. When this happens, expect the results to be painful and costly. Ruining a perfectly good piece of steel or sustaining a physical injury can both be avoided.

In the Loveless shop, two types of stainless steel – ATS-34 and BG-42 – are the primary selections. Bob will tell you, however, that those are not necessarily the most advantageous choices for a beginner. "Both ATS-34 and BG-42 can be challenging to work with, even for an experienced knife maker. Furthermore, heat treating either steel is best accomplished by an outside shop that specializes in that process," Loveless said.

spring steel, used for automobile leaf springs, is both inexpensive and forgiving when it comes to grinding and heat treatment. This steel usually comes in 1/4-inch thickness, but other thicknesses are available. A local flat spring manufacturer (offer to purchase the "cut-offs"), or cutlery supply retailer will be the best choice for new flat stock that comes already annealed.

5160: Blade Steel for Novices

In all likelihood, the first knife Bob Loveless ever made was crafted from 5160 spring steel. This steel is used for a wide variety of automobile springs and can be found in any junkyard, and a junkyard is where Loveless obtained his first piece of steel.

The chemistry and quality of 5160 can vary from steel mill to steel mill, so if the steel source is a junkyard, you'll never know what you have. That said, if you are able to acquire high-quality 5160 (often more by accident than on purpose) and use proven knife making methods, the steel performance will approach that of high quality 52100, the preferred steel of many knowledgeable knife makers.

5160 is a great steel for new makers for three reasons: it's readily available from a wide variety of sources; it's affordable for someone just starting out learning to make a knife; and when a high-quality version of the steel is combined with proven knife making skill, you can expect a corresponding outcome.

(opposite) After cleaning the flat steel stock, you'll need to scribe a pattern. Simply copy the shape of any fixed-blade knife onto a piece of white paper. (Image: Durwood Hollis)

For the beginner knife maker, the most practical approach to steel selection is to use one of the simple carbon steels. For example, 5160

The most readily available source of used automobile springs will be the local junk yard or vehicle parts recycler. If this is going to be your approach to blade steel, realize that the springs must be annealed prior to use. Annealing is a simple two-step process. Use a propane torch to heat the steel to a non-magnetic state, approximately 1,400-degrees Fahrenheit. Then, plunge the steel into a container of Vermiculite (available at nursery supply outlets) and let it come to room temperature (overnight). Afterwards, the steel will be annealed and ready to work.

In the beginning

After you've obtained a useable length of steel, it's important to clean the mill scale off of the flat stock with a file or belt grinder. Since you'll want a clean surface upon which to scribe your knife pattern, abrade the steel until it's bright and shiny.

"When I first started making knives, I worked directly with hot-rolled stock without removing the scale. Many times during heat-treating the blade blank would warp. However, when I started removing the mill scale, warping was less of problem," Loveless said.

If you purchase your flat stock from a knife supply shop, it will most likely be clean. Sometimes it's difficult to see a scribed line on even clean stock. For that reason, some makers paint the stock with a steel blue that provides for easy visualization of any mark.

Making a blade pattern

A blade pattern can be made by copying the shape of any knife onto a piece of heavy-weight paper. Lay the paper on flat surface and place whatever knife you want to replicate on top of the paper. For the purpose of this book we'll be using a Loveless drop-point (dropped hunter) knife for our pattern. Using a sharp pencil, draw around the knife so that its outline is copied onto the paper. Making several photocopies of the finished pattern is a good idea. Use a pair of scissors and cut out the paper pattern. Indicate on the pattern the position of the guard, handle rivets and lanyard hole (if any), so these can be marked onto the steel stock.

Scribing the pattern onto the blade stock

Place the pattern on top of the steel stock (some makers glue the pattern to the steel and grind to it). You'll need to hold it securely (using a clamp is good insurance against slippage) and scribe around the margin of the pattern with a sharp pointed marker or steel awl. Use enough pressure so that the outline is sharp and easily discernible. Also mark where the guard and handle rivets will be placed, as well as the lanyard hole. The end result should provide the complete outline of the knife on the steel stock.

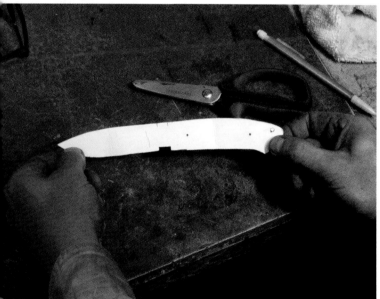

(top) When you've drawn out your pattern (blade, guard and handle), use scissors and cut it out. (Image: Durwood Hollis)

(middle) After the pattern has been cut from the paper, make sure you indicate the position of the guard and the handle rivet holes. (Image: Durwood Hollis)

(bottom) Tape the paper pattern on a piece of heavy construction paper or light cardboard and cut it out. This way, you'll have a heavier pattern that can be used over and over. (Image: Durwood Hollis)

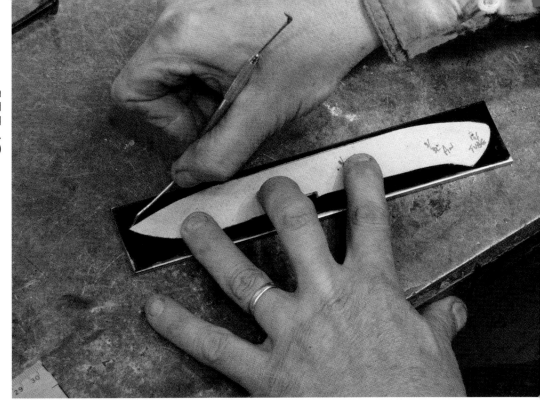

Place the pattern on the flat steel stock and scribe a line around the entire perimeter. (Image: Durwood Hollis)

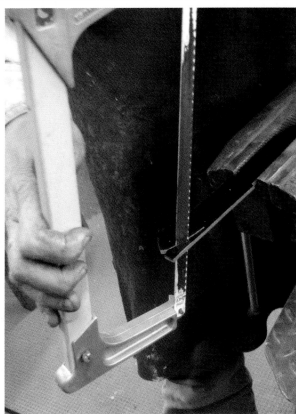

(left) A bandsaw will make the work of cutting out the blade blank a lot easier. If you have access to a belt grinder, that can also be used. (Image: Durwood Hollis)

(above) While a bandsaw is preferable, a hacksaw can also be used to cut out the blade blank. (Image: Durwood Hollis)

Cutting or grinding the blade blank

A belt grinder or a metal bandsaw, running about 50-80 SFPM (surface feet per minute), can be used to cut out the blade blank. A hacksaw can also be used to accomplish this task, but make sure you have lots of extra blades. In the Loveless shop a belt grinder is the tool of choice for this work. The idea is to remove anything than isn't the knife blade. Like the worker who sculpts an image from stone, you must free the blade from what holds it captive.

Grinding the blade outline is serious work. Loveless uses a 60-grit belt on the grinder for this activity. Starting at the butt of the steel stock, the excess material is removed to within 1/16 inch of the layout line. Exercise patience as you work and move progressively around the perimeter of the blade. Curves can be difficult. Drifting the belt to one side or the other will assist when working with tight curves.

When the blade blank is roughed out nearly to the margin of the layout line, it's time to change the grinder belt. Use a new 60-grit belt, or a 120, which is less aggressive. When you get close, lighten up on the pressure so you can see the layout line evaporate. Once you've carefully worked around the perimeter of the blank, this is the point where you'll want to stop. Now it's time to change to a 220-grit belt and carefully grind around the outside edge of the blank once again until you have a completely smooth surface.

Make your mark

After you have a blade blank in hand, use a center scribing tool (available from knife supply co.) to scribe a center line along the mid-point of the steel thickness in what will eventually become the cutting edge. Also, scribe lines on either side of the blade blank that correspond to the edge zone. These lines should be inset 1/16 to 1/8 inch from the edge of the blank. Both sets of lines will serve as a guide when the blank is bevel-ground.

The actual finished blade will be 3-1/2 inches in length, with a cutting edge of 3-1/4 inches. The 1/4 to 3/8-inch difference between blade length and cutting edge will become the flat ricasso (the unsharpened portion of the blade, just ahead of the guard). When you mark the edge zone bevel, it will be the same length as the final cutting edge. While you're marking lines on the blank, go ahead and mark the position of the ricasso, plunge cuts and the guard (each 3/8-inch wide) making sure both sides are the same dimension top and bottom.

Prior to additional shaping, the handle scale fastener holes and lanyard tube hole (optional) should be drilled. It's best to done this on a drill press because of the more

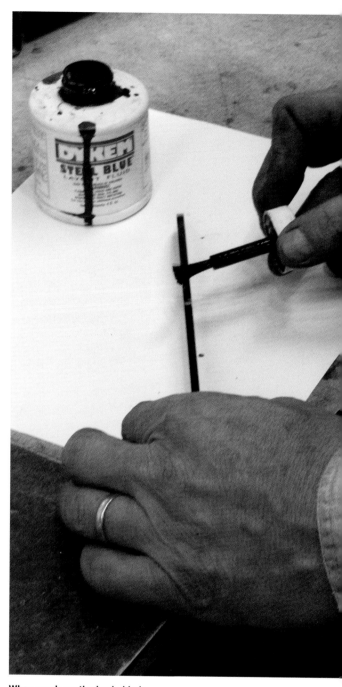

When you have the basic blade blank cut out, it is suggested that you apply a coat of steel blue to the eventual edge zone. This way you'll be able to easily see the initial edge bevel. (Image: Durwood Hollis)

precise nature of the drill presentation. However, a hand drill can be employed as long as the drill is carefully held at a 90-degree angle from the blank. Before drilling, use a center punch to mark each starting point. Typically, cutlery rivets are 5/16 inch in diameter, brass pins measure 1/8 inch in diameter and lanyard tubes are .257 inch in diameter. To make the rivet placement more precise, the use of a two-step cutlery rivet drill (available from knife supply dealers) or counter-bore tool can be advantageous.

Bevel and taper

Next, grind/file a 45-degree bevel on the cutting edge of the blank. This serves as a guide when you start grinding/filing the main blade taper. This also provides a lead-in bevel when you begin tapering the body of the blade. If you're using a belt grinder, without the lead-in

(above) Using a belt grinder simplifies creating an appropriate edge bevel. (Image: Durwood Hollis)

(right) Absent a belt grinder, you can always use a file to create the edge bevel. (Image: Durwood Hollis)

bevel on the blank, you'll remove a lot of abrasive from the grinding belt and this will slow your progress. Remember, always grind/file with the blade edge up. You'll be able to see the previously scribed center and edge zone lines more easily.

Even though it's not critical to taper the full tang of a fixed blade knife, by so doing you achieve better finished knife balance in the hand. Tapering the tang will remove excess weight from the handle. You can also drill a series of holes in the tang for the same purpose and avoid grinding/filing the tang altogether. Tapering the tang, however, provides grinding/filing experience that will serve you well when working on the main body of the blade. Any slight mistake made here is hidden beneath the handle scales. A grinding or filing error on the blade is clearly visible for all to see.

Prior to starting work on the tang, you'll need to grind/file a small starting bevel to lessen initial contact damage to the belt. Working slowly and methodically, continuously grind/file a taper from top to bottom and from the butt forward to just short of where the guard will be positioned. The objective here is to remove as much stock as possible from the tang to achieve a midpoint finished knife balance (rather than butt heavy).

(above) Tapering the tang demands good eye-hand coordination. Using a file can be real work, but with patience you can taper both sides of the blade blank equally. (Image: Durwood Hollis)

(left) Here the blade blank has been attached to a magnet, making it easier to hold at an angle while tapering the tang with a belt grinder. (Image: Durwood Hollis)

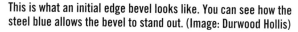

This is what an initial edge bevel looks like. You can see how the steel blue allows the bevel to stand out. (Image: Durwood Hollis)

(left) The tang has been tapered on both sides. (Image: Durwood Hollis)

(bottom) Tapering the blade will take patience and perseverance. Work slowly and carefully. (Image: Durwood Hollis)

(below) Fully tapered and profiled, the blade is now ready for heat-treat. (Image: Durwood Hollis)

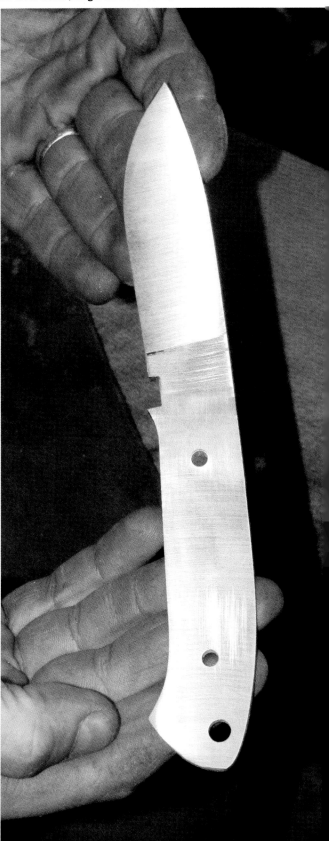

Grinding/filing blade tapers

If you're using a belt grinder, a fresh 60-grit belt is employed. Begin free-hand grinding, with your elbows braced against your ribcage. Your main hand should guide the work, while the off-side hand provides support. You will be flat grinding/filing the blank so it's tapered from top-to-bottom, meeting the original 45-degree edge zone bevel.

The primary objective of this effort should be total symmetry, from top to bottom and blade point to ricasso (flat area just ahead of the guard which lies outside of the main blade taper). Grind/file the plunge cut (termination point for the cutting edge) vertically from blade edge to back. When the tapering has been rough-finished, then change to a new 220-grit belt and smooth out the surface of the blade. You'll want to remove any deep scratches that could cause problems (stress risers) during heat treatment.

To the fire

Heat treatment of the annealed blade blank is a process whereby the physical properties of the steel are altered. The microstructure of the steel consists of tiny crystals called grains. The grain size and composition is what determines how well the blade retains its edge integrity. Each type of steel has its own optimal heat treatment schedule devised by metallurgists, and many of these processes include repeated thermal

cycles, multiple quenches and tempering.

Heat treating 5160 spring is a fairly simple undertaking. A propane torch is an adequate heat source for this procedure, and wearing heavy gloves will prevent accidental burns. The blade blank is suspended on a wire hanger and heated until it thoroughly reaches a non-magnetic state (approximately 1,450-degrees). This can

Files/abrasives

If you're not using a belt grinder, then an assortment of files will be needed for blade tapering. For initial rough work, an 8 to 10-inch-long Bastard Mill file is the best choice. An 8-inch half-round file will be necessary for any radius work. And an assortment of smaller files for cleaning up deep scratches will come in handy. Beyond this, wet/dry sandpaper will be used for polishing. Start with 100-grit, work your way up to at least 400-grit. Depending on what kind of finish you want to achieve, the blade can be hand-rubbed to 800-grit, or as far as 2000-grit.

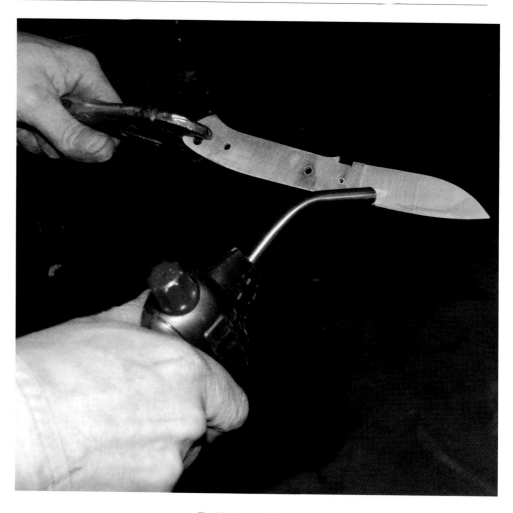

The blade should be hung on a wire or clamped into locking pliers for safety. A propane torch can be used to heat the blade to a non-magnetic state (bright red). (Image: Durwood Hollis)

(top left) After heating and quenching the blade blank, use a rag and some acetone to clean the steel.

(above) To prevent brittleness, you'll need to use low heat for a period of time. You can use your cooking oven, or a specialized heat-treat oven as pictured here. (Image: Durwood Hollis)

(left) After the completion of heat treatment, use ascending grades of abrasives to polish the blade. (Image: Durwood Hollis)

To even out the finish, consider using a buffing wheel and an appropriate grade of polishing compound to complete the blade finish. (Image: Durwood Hollis)

be judged by testing with a magnet. When this has been accomplished, immediately quench the blade in old motor oil, transmission fluid or your own concoction. This will serve to transform the austenite within the blade to a fine, hard crystalline structure called martensite. Furthermore, the quench stabilizes the size of the individual grains (crystals) within the steel.

While martensite is extremely hard, it's also quite brittle. If not properly tempered, the blade will chip and easily break. Tempering is where the kitchen oven comes in handy. Preheat the oven to 350 degrees Fahrenheit (use an in-oven thermometer, don't depend on the external control knob). While you're waiting for the oven to heat up, clean the blade blank with lacquer thinner or acetone to remove any trace of the quenching fluid. This will keep your oven clean and cut down on the smoke. Leave the blade blank in the oven to "soak" for two hours. After the completion of the tempering cycle, remove the blade and cool at room temperature overnight.

Making and fitting the guard

It isn't necessary to affix a guard to a knife. Many knives, including some very expensive custom models, are made without this feature. "I like a guard purely for its safety feature. The guard keeps the knife user's forefinger from accidentally slipping forward onto the sharpened blade edge. Should that happen, a serious injury could result," Loveless said.

A guard is nothing more than a cross-member piece, affixed to the forward end of the handle, next to the ricasso. There are many types of guards, but the single guard is one of the most attractive. The Loveless-style single guard is flush with the back of the blade and extends below the ricasso approximately 3/8-inch. While you can use stainless steel and nickel-silver for guard material, brass is easier to work with and less expensive.

If the steel you're working with is 3/8-inch thick, then the dimensions of the finished guard are as follows: 1-1/4 inches in length, 3/8 inch wide, with a thickness of 3/8 inch. To make the guard, you'll need to cut a piece of flat brass stock slightly larger in overall size. Scribe a center line down both the lengths (this will allow precision placement of the pins), as well as down the thickness (this provides a guide for making a slot so the guard can simply slide onto the ricasso).

Select a drill bit slightly smaller than the blade slot you'll want cut out from the guard. Since the blade at the tang/ricasso is 3/16-inch thick, I suggest using a 9/64-inch drill bit. Use a center punch to start a line of holes that will eventually be filed into an elongated slot. Drill the line of holes close together, and then remove the ma-

(below) After you've cut out the guard blank, scribe a centerline and indicate on that line where the bottom of the guard meets the bottom of the blade blank. (Image: Durwood Hollis)

(bottom) Use a center punch to create a series of starter holes. (Image: Durwood Hollis)

(left) Drill a series of holes in the guard blank that will eventually form a slot to accept the blade blank. (Image: Durwood Hollis)

(below right) 26 A hacksaw can be used to cut out the guard slot that was started with the series of drill holes. (Image: Durwood Hollis)

(below left) When you've cut the initial guard slot, place the guard blank in a vise and use a file to clean up the cut. Don't file too much. Try-fit the guard at various points as you work. (Image: Durwood Hollis)

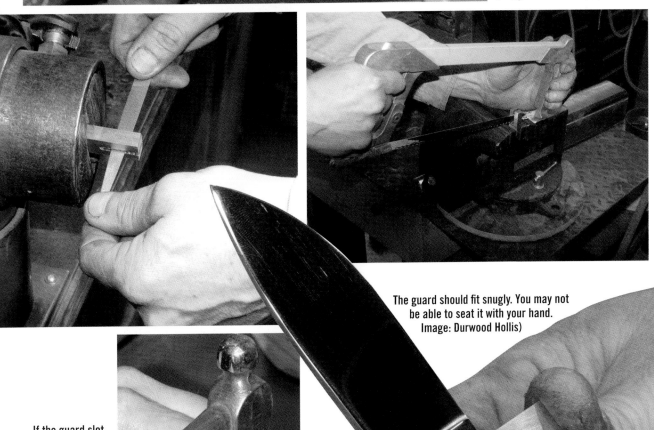

The guard should fit snugly. You may not be able to seat it with your hand. Image: Durwood Hollis)

If the guard slot has been properly cut, then it will take a few taps from a hammer to seat it into position. (Image: Durwood Hollis)

terial that remains between each hole with a small file. Work slowly and try-fit the guard several times, so you end up with a tight fit when the guard is secured onto the tang/ricasso. If you've done the job right, the guard will fit snugly and stay there.

Next, clamp the guard in place and, using the previously scribed center line, locate two evenly spaced points for attachment pin holes. Center-punch both holes and drill with a bit the same diameter as the pins. When you're finished drilling, try-fit both pins to hold the guard firmly in place. At this point, you can rough out the final shape of the guard. Afterward, remove the guard and the blade is ready for heat-treating.

Hammer time

Guard attachment can be done either before or after polishing. If you've made the guard fit the tang properly, there should be no gap between the two. A tight fit can be interpreted as needing light hammer taps to position the guard on the tang. If the guard has been

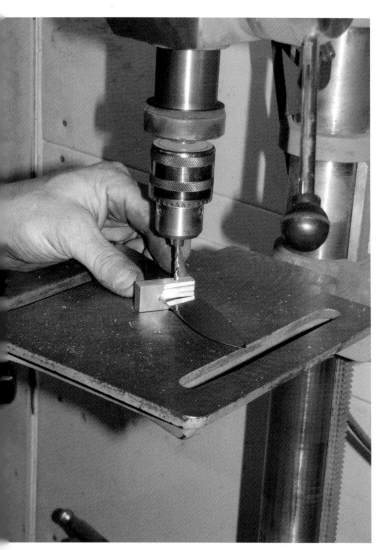

(left) Center punch and drill a guard retaining pin hole through the guard and the blade blank. After the hole has been drilled, slightly counter-bore on both sides of the guard.

(above) Slide the brass retaining pin through the hole, cut to an appropriate length and peen both sides. (Image: Durwood Hollis)

properly fitted, the pins alone will prevent any guard movement and eliminate the need for soldering.

Counter-bore external pin holes slightly on both sides of the guard. This allows the pins to be hammered in such a way that they form a rivet to securely hold the guard in place. Cut the pins so they are slightly longer than the guard itself (about 1/2 the diameter of the pin itself). This way the pins will mushroom down, rather than bending over. When hammering, alternate working on either side of the guard so that the pin heads are equally mushroomed.

Polish

Once the blade blank has been adequately heat treated, the next step is to make sure that it remained absolutely flat. During heat treatment the blade blank can warp slightly. The only way to achieve true flatness at this stage is to regrind the tang with a new 60-grit belt, or do some serious filing.

After the blade has been checked for straightness, use a new 220-grit belt and grind both sides and the edges to finish size and thickness. Be sure to remove any deep scratches. If you don't remove them now, they'll be quite visible as the polishing procedure continues (smaller files can also be used to clean up the scratches, and various grit sizes of wet/dry sandpaper will work as a polishing agent). Next, switch to a 440-grit belt to smooth out any remaining scratches. Last of all, a 500-grit extra-flexible belt is used to finish the polish. The end result should be a smooth and shiny blade that's completely scratch-free.

Time for a break

It has taken a lot of hard work to get to this point. You've taken a piece of steel stock, scribed a blade pattern on it and removed everything that doesn't look like a knife. The blade has been profiled and a single guard attached. And there've been lots of calo-ries expended grinding/filing/polishing the blade. However, there's still more to be accomplished. The handle scales have to be selected, cut to size, affixed to the tang and shaped. And that will be the next phase of the knife building process.

Knife kits

All of the initial cutting, filing, grinding and heat-treatment involved in producing a blade blank can be challenging to the beginning knife maker. The same can be said about guard manufacture and soldering. For those who are somewhat reluctant to jump into a knife making project, using a knife kit with a pre-soldered guard might be the way to go. With a kit, all of the tough work is already done for you. The preformed blade (all of the grinding steps have already been completed), with a guard soldered in place, handle material and pins are all part of the kit. Easier still, there are kits available with a blade that doesn't need a guard. And all of the other components, including a sheath, are part of the package. Also, DVDs are available that depict the entire kit knife making process step-by-step. Even those with limited manual skill and simple hand tools can put together a nice looking knife. For information on dealers that offer knife kits for sale, turn to the resource guide in the final chapter of this book.

STEEL SENSE

Steel in its basic form is nothing more than iron alloyed with a small percentage of carbon. Other alloying elements can be added that provide a variety of properties to the steel. To assist in your understanding of these elements and their properties the following is provided:

BLADE STEEL ALLOY PROPERTIES

ELEMENT	PROPERTIES
Carbon (C)	Increases hardness, improves resistance to wear and abrasion
Chromium (Cr)	Increases hardness, tensile strength and toughness
Cobalt (Co)	Increases tensile strength, hardness and intensifies the effect of other elements
Copper (Cu)	Increases corrosion and wear resistance
Manganese (Mn)	Increases hardness, wear resistance and tensile strength
Molybdenum (Mo)	Increases hardness, tensile strength and toughness
Nickel (Ni)	Adds strength, hardness and corrosion resistance
Phosphorous (P)	Enhances strength, machinability and hardness
Silicon (Si)	Increases yield strength, hardness and machinabilty
Sulphur (S)	In small quantities, this element improves machinability
Tungsten (W)	Adds strength, hardness and toughness
Vanadium (V)	Reduces grain growth and Increases strength, hardness and resistance to impact

NON~STAINLESS BLADE STEELS

This selection of non-stainless blade steels is limited to those most commonly encountered in domestic custom and production cutlery.

NON-STAINLESS BLADE STEELS, CONTAINED ALLOY PERCENTAGE

Steel	Carbon	Manganese	Chromium	Nickel	Vanadium	Molybdenum	Tungsten	Cobalt
O-1	0.85-1.00	1.00-1.40	0.40-0.60	0.30	0.30			
1095	0.90-1.03	0.30-0.50						
5160	0.56-0.64	0.75-1.00	0.70-0.90					
52100	0.98-1.10	0.25-0.45	1.30-1.60					
A-2	0.95-1.05	1.00	4.75-5.50	0.30	0.15-0.50	0.90-1.40		
D-2	1.40-1.60	0.60	11.00-13.00	0.30	1.10	0.70-1.20		

NON-STAINLESS BLADE STEEL CHARACTERISTICS

Each steel formulation has its own characteristics, which are derived from the presence of various alloying elements. While non-stainless blade steels will rust if not cared for properly, nevertheless, they all make fine edged tools.

O-1: While this steel is moderately wear-resistant and tough, it offers little corrosion-resistance and easily develops a patina when exposed to acidic materials (food, stomach acid, etc.).

1095: This steel has elevated carbon content and its strength can be found in toughness and ductility. Often used in machetes and various tactical knives.

5160: A spring steel that is used in automobile leaf springs. Easy for the beginning knife maker to work with and heat-treat at home.

52100: High-carbon steel with a smidgen of chromium and manganese. Used in ball bearings and bearing races, it is a very fine grain steel that offers good edge retention, wear resistance and toughness.

A-2: This is air-hardened steel that is very tough and wear resistant. However, edge retention and impact resistance cannot be compared to other high-performance stainless formulations. Its real asset is that the steel is easy to work and as such is a good choice for the beginning knife maker.

D-2: Even though this steel has high chromium content, it is not stainless. It can, however, be considered highly stain-resistant. The steel is extremely wear resistant due to the elevated levels of carbon, chromium and molybdenum.

STAINLESS BLADE STEELS

This selection of blade steels is limited to those most often encountered in domestic custom and production cutlery. Interestingly, many of these formulations have a great deal of similarity (eg.154CM/ATS34, 440 series/AUS series and ZDP-189/Cowry-X).

STAINLESS BLADE STEELS, CONTAINED ALLOY PERCENTAGE

Steel	Carbon	Manganese	Chromium	Nickel	Vanadium	Molybdenum	Tungsten	Cobalt
420HC	0.40-0.50	0.8	12.00-14.00		0.18	0.6		
440A	0.65-0.75	1.0	16.00-18.00			0.75		
440B	0.75-0.95	1.0	16.00-18.00			0.75		
440C	0.95-1.20	1.0	16.00-18.00			0.75		
AUS-6	0.55-0.65	1.0	13.00-14.50	0.49	0.10-0.25			
AUS-8	0.70-0.75	0.5	13.00-14.50	0.49	0.10-0.26	0.10-0.30		
AUS-10	0.95-1.10	0.50	13.00-14.50	0.49	0.10-0.27	0.10-0.31		
12C27	0.60	0.40	13.5					
154CM	1.05	0.50	14.00			4.0		
ATS34	1.05	0.40	14.00			4.0		
ATS55	1.00	0.50	14.00			0.60		0.40
VG-10	0.95-1.05	0.50	14.50-15.50		0.10-0.30	0.90-1.20		1.30-1.50
BG-42	1.15	0.50	14.50		1.20	4.00		
CPMS30V	1.45		14.00		4.0	2.00		
CPMS90V	2.30		14.00		9.00	1.00		
ZDP-189	3.0		20.00					
Cowry-X	3.0		20.00		0.30	1.00		
Stellite 6K	1.90	2.00	32.00	3.00		1.50	4.50	64.00
Talonite 6BH	0.90	2.00	28.0-32.0	3.00		1.50	4.50	64.00
H-1	0.15	2.00	14.00-16.00	6.00-8.00		0.50-1.50		

The most important feature of stainless formulations is that they are highly resistant to environmental invectives. However, neglecting to care for a stainless blade can result in the formation of rust. When selecting a stainless steel to build a knife, realize that to get a particular characteristic, in most instances another is sacrificed. And heat-treatment and cryogenic tempering of stainless steels are best undertaken by professionals experienced with those processes.

420HC: Due to the fact that this steel possesses a solid combination of edge retention, sharpening ease and corrosion-resistance, it is a popular production cutlery material.

440A: Since this steel provides high corrosion resistance and affordability, it is often used in entry-level production cutlery.

440B: The slightly higher carbon content of this steel offers better wear resistance than 440A, but it is rarely used in either custom or production cutlery.

440C: A step up over its other 400 series brethren, this steel offers increased hardness and wear resistance.

AUS-6: The carbon content of this steel is somewhat lower than 440A, but the vanadium component, which is absent in 440A, allows for slightly higher hardness and better wear resistance. Otherwise, this material and 440A are quite similar.

AUS-8: There is considerable similarity between this material and 440B. While the carbon content is slightly lower than 440B, the addition of both nickel and vanadium allow this material to achieve slightly higher hardness values. Most users can't tell the difference between this steel and 440B.

AUS-10: While this material has less chromium than 440C, the added nickel in the chemical formulation provides similar corrosion resistance. Also, the vanadium component offers enhanced wear resistance over 440C.

12C27: Produced by Sandvik, this is an extremely clean stainless that combines corrosion resistance, toughness and edge retention in a quality product.

154CM: This steel has slightly less chromium and slightly more molybdenum than 440C stainless. Many consider the steel an upgrade from 440C. It offers high edge retention, but can be a touch brittle.

ATS34: This material is virtually the same as 154CM, with a tiny amount of manganese removed from the chemical makeup.

ATS55: The addition of vanadium to this steel formulation provides enhanced edge retention over ATS34.

VG-10: This high-carbon stainless is somewhat similar to 154CM. However, the addition of vanadium and cobalt give it better edge retention and corrosion-resistance.

BG-42: This steel is used in ball bearings and is highly resistant to both heat and wear. Significant increases in both vanadium and molybdenum give it the edge over 154CM.

CPMS30V: Produced by particle (powder) metallurgy, this steel has a high-carbon, high-vanadium content. This steel is easier to grind/file than S90V due to lower vanadium content than other related CPM powder steels. For the same reason, however, the steel also has a lower measure of wear resistance.

CPMS90V: Also produced by particle metallurgy, this steel is a step up in wear resistance and corresponding edge retention over S30V. This is due to additional carbon and a huge dose of vanadium in the chemical composition.

ZDP-189: A steel of Japanese origin, it is produced by powder metallurgy. The main feature is that it can be taken to a very high Rockwell hardness (RC 66-67), which provides increased edge retention. The chemical composition is very similar to Cowry-X.

Cowry-X: Particle metallurgy steel from Japan that has an extremely high carbon and chromium content. Both of these assets allow for very high hardness (Rc 65-67) and outstanding edge retention. This steel is quite similar in chemical composition to ZDP-189.

Talonite: This is a non-magnetic cobalt alloy. It is most useful when extreme corrosion-resistance is sought. However, it is very soft (Rc 42-47) and edge retention is far less than many of the high-carbon stainless steels.

Stellite: Another cobalt-chromium alloy that is similar to Talonite. While the cobalt component is non-magnetic and provides toughness, additional carbon in the chemical makeup of this material imparts superior wear resistance over Talonite.

H-1: This is age-hardened steel that is very corrosion-resistant. However, edge retention is only comparable to the less wear-resistant stainless formulations.

R.W. Loveless
maker
Riverside, Calif.
220
R.W. LOVELESS
maker
Riverside, Calif.

(top) An unusual knife in that it features a duplex grind. Very few with this type of blade grind were made in the Loveless shop. (bottom) This knife was the prototype model for the duplex hunter shown above. It features a 4" blade, stainless steel bolster and pins and a maroon Micarta handle.

R.W. LOVELESS
maker
Riverside, Calif.

This skinner features half tang construction and bears Loveless's Riverside logo.

This whittler combines a 2-3/8" Wharncliff-style blade with a sheep horn handle and the Loveless Riverside logo. Interestingly, the handle turns up, rather than down, at its terminus.

R.W. LOVELESS
maker
Riverside, Calif.

An interesting Loveless creation that features a
3" modified drop-point blade, a half tang and a
stiff horn handle with an engraved bolster.

CHAPTER FIVE

Handle Work

BLADE PERFORMANCE, USER COMFORT AND SAFETY ALL DEPEND ON HANDLE DESIGN

If you've ever flown in a small plane and watched the pilot handle the controls, then you know how important it is to have mastery over the mechanics that keep the aircraft aloft. I believe that feeling of being in control is the most intoxicating element of flying. Absent control, peril awaits.

While a knife may not have the multiple control surfaces of an aircraft, it does have a handle. And that single element directs the cutting edge. Optimal knife performance depends on how well the user can control the force directed into the blade by the hand. To accomplish this, the handle must conform to the grip pocket of the hand.

Ergonomics is the science that studies the relationship between humans and their work activities. The term "ergonomics" comes from two Greek words, ergon (work) and nomos (natural law). To create an ergonomic, or user-friendly, knife handle, the maker must first realize that no two persons are the same. Furthermore, every cutting activity, no matter how similar, will have some significant differences.

Recently, a production cutlery firm has made their own version of an ergonomic-handled hunting knife. What they've done is put a slight swell on the right side of the knife handle. Basi-

cally, this is nothing more than a clone of the palm swell seen on some rifle stocks. While this type handle fits the grip pocket of the right hand, it leaves left-handed folks out of the picture.

Even though a small percentage (12-15%) of us are left-handed, creating a knife handle that only fits right-handers means that to fit the rest of the population you have to create two different knives. A better approach is to design an ambidextrous handle that fits everyone.

The final job in our knife building project is attaching and shaping the handle scales. This procedure involves a number of steps and a bit of artistic flare. When done with patience and care, the result will allow us mastery over the blade performance. (Image: Durwood Hollis)

Even though Bob Loveless is right-handed, he understood the need for an ambidextrous knife handle early in his knife making career. "A knife needs to fit the hand – either hand. The best design to do that is a flattened oval, or an elliptical handle tapered at both ends," Loveless said. The Loveless-style knife handle is just that. It's slightly fatter at the mid-point, with the forward end sloping into the guard and the back end tapering to the lanyard hole where it swells slightly toward the handle terminus.

According to Loveless, "My knife handles will naturally fit anybody because they were designed with the interior of the human hand in mind. A knife handle should feel friendly in your hand," he said. Indeed, when you hold a Loveless knife, there isn't any need to make physical adjustments. The shape of the handle is such that it meets the ergonomic demands of the hand. And all of this from a knife maker who didn't graduate from high school.

Getting started

Basically, there are two types of fixed-blade knife handles: full-tang (handle scales are attached to either

When you've decided on a particular type of handle material (in this case, desert ironwood), make sure that all surfaces of the handle scales are flat and square. (Image: Durwood Hollis)

side of the tang) and hidden tang (the tang is concealed within the handle material). While Loveless has made and will continue to make a few hidden-tang knives, his preference is full-tang knives. In this chapter, we'll focus on constructing a full-tang knife with external handle scales.

When you purchase handle scale material, each piece of the matched set it (you'll need two pieces, one for each side of the full-length tang) will be approximately 3/8 inch thick. For a hidden tang-handle you'll need a solid piece of material. With either type of handle, this leaves plenty of material to ergonomically shape the grip surface. The shape isn't dramatic, but enough so that the handle can be easily gripped by the hand. Because each side of the handle duplicates the shape of the other, the knife can be used in either hand.

Full-tang knife handle

Hopefully, you've already selected a pair of handle scales (see the section on handle material at the end of this chapter). Lay the one scale down on a flat surface and draw the outline of the tang. Set that scale aside. Flip the blade over and do the same thing on the other scale. Make sure that the edge that fits up against the rear of the tang is straight.

Place the blade tang flat on one scale and make sure it's snug against the guard. Trace the outline of the tang on the handle scale. (Image: Durwood Hollis)

(left) After you've traced the outline of the tang on the handle scale, remove all of the excess material. This can be done by grinding, filing or using a bandsaw (pictured). Repeat this with the opposite side of the blade tang. (Image: Durwood Hollis)

(below) If you've decided to use a colored spacer, trace the outline of the handle scale on the material. (Image: Durwood Hollis)

(bottom) Once you have traced the outline of the handle scale on the colored spacer material, cut the spacer out. You'll have to repeat this procedure for the opposite side of the blade tang. (Image: Durwood Hollis)

After you've drawn the outline of the blade tang on the handle scales, remove excess material with a belt grinder (Loveless uses a Clausing Vertical Mill), bandsaw, or with a flat bastard file, to approximately 1/8 inch of the tang. When you're finished, check the fit and make any final adjustment. What you want to end up with is a tight fit between tang, spacer and scales.

If you're going to add a fiber space to the full-tang knife handle (optional), then your first job will be to decide on the color. Fortunately, a wide color selection of spacer material is available from knife supply outlets. Once you have the spacer material in hand, lay it down on a flat surface and trace the outline of the blade tang with a marker. Remember, make sure you have a totally straight edge where the spacer will eventually butt up against the rear of the guard. Don't forget there are two sides to the tang, so draw one side, flip the blade over and repeat for the other side

After you've drawn the outline of the blade tang on the spacer material, it's time to cut it out. Loveless uses a pair of straight-cut aviation sheet metal shears for this job. However, any kind of heavy-duty shears, or a bandsaw will do. Once you've cut out both spacers, check the fit and make any necessary adjustments.

Once you have the handle scales and colored spacers ground or filed to size, it's time to epoxy the handle components together. There are multiple sources for epoxy, including your local hardware store and knife supply outlets. Regardless of brand, all of this stuff works the same, more or less. Epoxy comes in two separate parts. It works as an adhesive when the two are mixed in correct proportions to each other. Mix the two together either in a small throw-away container, or on something smooth and disposable (plastic container lid).

Use a small stiff brush to thoroughly coat the inner side of the near-handle scale. Then coat the inner side of the colored spacer with epoxy and position them on the

knife tang, taking care to line everything up just right. Now that the near-side is glued-up, the next step is to drill holes for the pins and lanyard tube (optional). Using the pin and lanyard tube holes in the tang as a guide (as detailed in the previous chapter, pins are usually 5/16 inch and lanyard tubes are .257 inch in diameter, respectively), drill identical size holes in the spacer and scale.

Now that you have one side of the handle drilled, repeat the same procedure on the other side. Next, countersink the pin holes on the outside of each scale. The use of a two-step cutlery rivet drill (available at knife supply outlets) will make this job a lot more precise. Finally,

The handle scales and colored spacer will be attached to each other and the blade tang with epoxy. Mix the epoxy in something that can be disposed of after you're through using it.

(below) Thoroughly coat one side of the blade tang, both sides of the colored spacer and the inner side of the handle scale with epoxy. (Image: Durwood Hollis)

(bottom) Place the colored spacer on the blade tang, followed by the handle scales. (Image: Durwood Hollis)

press-fit the pins into their respective holes to keep the entire handle in one piece. Clamp everything together and use either a belt grinder or a file to bring the margins of the spacer and scales down to the tang.

(above) Clamp the handle scale and spacer to the blade tang and let the epoxy dry. (Image: Durwood Hollis)

(right) When the epoxy has dried, drill through the pin and lanyard holes in the blade tang to establish their position on the handle scale. When you've done that, repeat steps illustrated on pages 82 and 83 on the opposite side of the blade tang. (Image: Durwood Hollis)

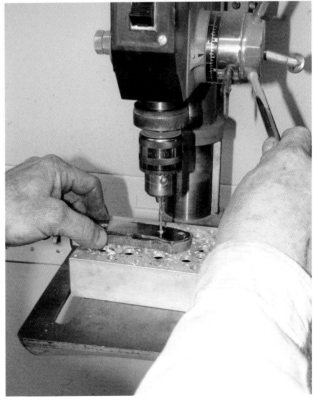

If you made provision in the tang for a lanyard hole, now is the time to seat the lanyard tube. Position the lanyard tube and tap it in so the far end is even with near handle scale. Now, it's time to epoxy that off-side colored spacer and place it down on the pins and lanyard tube, directly against the handle tang. When this done, coat the exposed surface of the colored washer with epoxy and position the off-side handle scale in place. Finally, peen the pins so that all of the handle components are snug in place and let dry overnight.

When the epoxy has completely dried, it's time

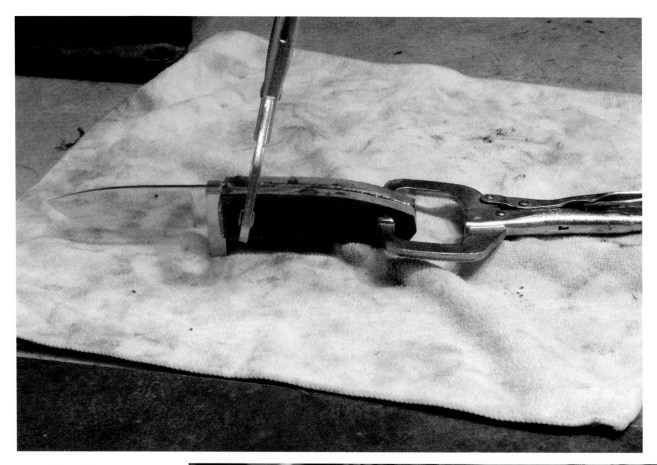

(above) Clamp both sides of the handle together and let the epoxy dry. (Image: Durwood Hollis)

(right) When the epoxy has dried and the handle scales are firmly attached to the blade tang, drill through the pin and lanyard holes so that you have through-and-through holes on both sides of the handle. Make sure you counter-bore the rivet/pin holes slightly on either side. (Image: Durwood Hollis)

(above) Insert the pins into the handle and tighten. (Image: Durwood Hollis)

(right) Insert the thong tube into the lanyard hole and peen on both sides. (Image: Durwood Hollis)

(below) A wood rasp or file can be used to shape the handle. Work slowly and carefully. (Image: Durwood Hollis)

(bottom right Here the maker is using disc sander to profile the handle scales. (Image: Durwood Hollis)

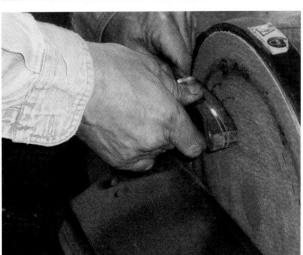

to finish shaping the handle. You can start out with a wood rasp (work slowly – these bad boys can remove a lot wood fast). While you're at it, shape the guard also. The use of a smaller rasp is recommended when working on that portion of the handle nearest to the guard. This will help you to avoid making deep scratches in the brass. In the Loveless shop a belt grinder is used to shape handle and the guard. Start out with a 40-grit belt, using care not to touch semi-finished tang and guard surfaces. Remember, it's easy to remove material, but impossible to put it back on again. Work slowly and remove small amounts at a time. Once the handle has been rough-shaped, switch to 220-grit to smooth up the surface.

All that's left now is a little detail work on the handle. Use a crossing file to touch up the area near the guard and the flared area of the lower butt. Now switch to narrow strips of

(left) Profiling the guard with a belt grinder is the easiest way to get the right shape, but you can also use a file. (Image: Durwood Hollis)

(below) When the guard and handle have been properly shaped, use ascending grades of abrasives to bring out the luster and shine of both components. (Image: Durwood Hollis)

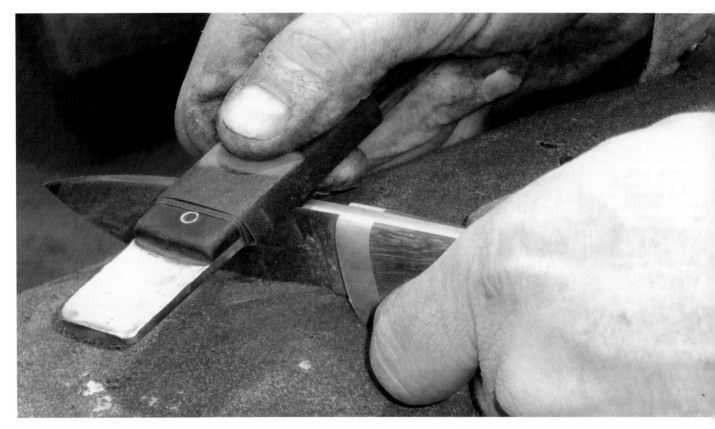

(above) The careful use of various grades of abrasive can be used to finish both the handle and the blade. Note that the maker has wrapped a strip of abrasive onto a narrow, flat piece of metal to provide consistent abrasive-to-material contact. (Image: Durwood Hollis)

(left) The use of a buffing wheel and abrasive compound will make applying the final finish a lot easier. However, a knife can be finished entirely by hand. (Image: Durwood Hollis)

(above) Here the maker has brought out the character of the handle with a final polish. (Image: Durwood Hollis)

(right) Here's the final product. All it needs now is a carrying sheath and it's ready for the field. (Image: Durwood Hollis)

emery cloth and go over the entire handle using what Loveless terms "a shoe shine motion." Start with 320-grit and then finish with 500- or 600-grit.

At this point, Loveless etches his trademark into the blade. He feels that stamping highly-stressed steel isn't a good thing. Of course, it's not an absolute necessity to mark the knife. Those who produce knives to sell use the mark to distinguish their work from other others. And stamping a trademark on the blade is common practice with many knife makers, both production and handmade. Since etching a trademark can be a complicated process for the beginner, an easier method is to purchase a maker's stamp (made to order with whatever you want on it), and stamp the riccaso.

When you've completed the knife, give it a final buffing to put a lustrous shine all over. This can be done by hand with 400-grit abrasive, followed by 600-grit abrasive. The abrasive paper will load-up quickly and must be changed often. Most makers use some form of push-stick/abrasive combination to exert more pressure on the steel and speed the work. Make sure when you're polishing the blade to work in one direction only. In this way, your effort with the abrasive will produce a uniform surface.

Hidden-tang knife handle

Note: The following hidden (narrow) tang handle procedures are included herein, but not illustrated. The reason for this is Bob Loveless' preferred handle construction method is full-tang with external handle scales. It is suggested that mastery of that method of handle attachment is a necessary step for any knife builder to master before attempting alternative handle attachment procedures.

The first step in this procedure is to lay-out the hidden tang blade pattern on paper. Once you have the design on paper, transfer it to the steel stock (see Chapter 4). The next step is cut out or grind out the blade pattern, using either a hack saw or a belt grinder (see Chapter 3). If you're using a hack saw, then keep the steel stock clamped tight against the jaws of the vise. When the distance of the work gets more than 1/2 to 3/4 of an inch away from the jaws, move the work and re-clamp. Saw out a rough outline and don't worry about being precise. All of the clean-up work can be accomplished with files. Just stay outside of the scribe lines.

Dealing with a hidden tang blade is similar to the full-tang version, with the exception of the merger between blade and tang. After you've profiled the blade (see Chapter 3), then it's time to deal with the tang. Where the ricasso drops down in width to meet the narrow tang, you'll want to use a half-round file to create a curved slope. This provides strength at the critical junction of blade and tang.

If we were to make this a right angle, thereby creating a stress riser, then the potential for breakage at that point is greatly increased. By sloping and curving this junction, the integrity of the blade is maintained. While the actual curve of the file surface doesn't exactly match the radius of the curve, this can be done by moving the file slightly while filing. When you have this roughed-out, then switch to a small round file to true-up the pattern.

There are several types of hidden tangs, as well a multitude of ways to join the handle to the tang. The simplest hidden tang approach for a beginning knife maker is to use a section of stag that provides adequate length for a handle. The best stag handle material comes from tropical deer species, especially Indian Sambar. Antler that comes from the various whitetail and mule deer species tends to be pithy in the middle and must have the end capped to cover the pithy interior. The internal structure of tropical deer antler is far more consistent. A section of Sambar stag, regardless of what part of the antler it is cut from, can be used by simply polishing end, thereby eliminating the need for a cap. The same is not true when North American deer antler is used. The only exception would be a crown section (that portion where the antler is joined to the skull) of the antler. The internal antler structure here tends to be solid enough to allow polishing.

Since the blade tang slopes down to 3/8-inch in width, you'll need to create a cavity in the center of the stag to accept the tang. And this cavity must be wide enough at the top to allow the tang shoulder to fit. Wrap the stag in a piece of scrap leather to protect the outer surface. Secure the stag perpendicular to the top of the vise. The length of the handle will be about 4-1/2 inches, however, the tang will be somewhat shorter. Even a 3-inch tang, when securely joined to the stag, is enough to support the blade.

Mark a vertical centerline on the end of the antler that you want to drill. Using a 3/8-in drill bit, make the first hole in the center of the antler. This hole should be as deep as the tang is long. Using the same drill bit, drill a series of holes on both sides of the center hole no deeper than the length of the curved tang shoulder. Using a rattail file, clean up the entire cavity and try-fit the tang. It may take considerable work to get the tang to fit right, but be patient and work slowly. Make sure the fit against the rear of the guard is square and tight. Once you have everything right, then it's time to epoxy the tang into the handle cavity.

Keeping the stag wrapped in leather, position it vertically (use a level) in the vise with the tang cavity up. Mix the epoxy and pour enough into the cavity to fill it within a short distance from the top. Next, insert the tang in the cavity (some makers drill a series of holes in the tang to allow the epoxy to flow through for a better hold). Use paper towels or a rag to wipe off any epoxy that overflows the joint between the guard and the stag. Make whatever adjustments necessary to ensure that the blade and handle are in line with one another and let the epoxy set.

Next, you'll want to taper the handle material to fit the rear of the guard. First, wrap the guard in a double layer of masking tape. Should you accidentally override the handle material, the masking tape will protect the smooth surface of the guard. Working slowly and parallel with the end of the guard, carefully file the handle material down at an angle until it nearly meets the rear of the guard. When you get close to guard, switch to fine grain wet/dry sand paper. In this way you'll be able to bring the leading edge of the handle in line with the rear of the guard, with nothing more than a fine line indicating the point where the two are joined.

You'll also need work on the end of the handle. With

a file, carefully remove surface material until you achieve a very slight domed shape. It you're using crown stag, there maybe a tiny amount of dried skin, hair or other debris attached at the pedicle. This can be removed with a wire brush. Since you can easily scratch the stag, don't overdo the brush work. When you've roughed the shape of the end of the handle out, switch to fine grain wet/dry sandpaper to achieve a smooth finish.

Near the pedicle (attachment to the skull). most stag will have several small to large projections from the surface. Since these will make gripping the handle uncomfortable, you'll want to file them down until they're smooth and consistent with the rest of the surface. If there's an eye guard, this can be cut-off with a hacksaw and then file down. If you're able to pick the particular piece of stag handle material, select the straightest and smoothest piece you can find. This will cut down on the detail work you have to do at this stage.

Alternate hidden tang approach

As stated at the outset, there is more than one way to make a hidden tang knife. One approach is to create a tang opening that runs the entire length of the handle material. To accomplish this, you'll have to select an extremely straight piece of stag, or if the stag is slightly curved the tang will have to be bent. My suggestion is the former, rather than the latter (less work). And this means selecting a section of antler, rather than a crown piece.

Once you have the tang cavity filed out to fit, the end of the tang will need a little work. A portion of the end will be threaded (about 1/2 inch), so taper the tang slightly toward the end. Clamp that section in the vise, tight to the jaws. Using a flat bastard file, round the portion of the tang to be threaded until it becomes a round rod. With the tang still clamped in the vise, thread the rounded end using plenty of thread cutting oil. Once the threading is complete, check for fit with the handle material. The end of the threaded portion of the tang should be flush with the end of the handle. Remove the tang and drill a hole into the end of the handle to countersink the nut that will be applied to the tang. This hole should be deep enough so that, when the handle is bolted up, the connecting round nut is countersunk into the butt cap.

With everything bolted together, you can work on the guard/handle connection. Again, wrap the guard in masking tape to protect it from accidental damage. The first thing you'll want to do is ensure that the leading end of the handle material is square with the rear of the guard. To do this, you may have to do a little file work

on the handle material. Next, use a flat file to taper the handle material down to match the shape of the rear of the guard. All of the close work should be done with wet/dry sandpaper, finishing off with a 400-grit abrasive for the final fit/polish.

You'll need a butt cap, so let's move on to that part of the project. The butt cap can be made from almost anything, but since the guard is brass, a matching brass butt cap is a good choice. Using the same 3/8-inch brass material that the guard was constructed of, cut out a square large enough to cover the end of the knife handle. In the center, drill a hole large enough to accept the threaded end of the tang. Obtain a round brass nut (check with any one of the knife supply outlets) and thread it onto the tang.

With the brass square securely fastened on to the end of the knife handle, use a sharp-pointed marking pen to trace the outline of the end of the handle. Remove the brass square, clamp it up in the vise and use a hack saw to rough out the outlined shape. When you have the basic shape cut out, use a file to do the finish work right to the line. Try-fit the butt cap and make any final adjustments to achieve a perfect fit with the handle.

Now, it's time to bond the handle components together with epoxy and bolt them tight. Wrap the blade in a scrap piece of leather and clamp it vertically in the vise. Mix the epoxy and coat the surface of the tang and the underside of the guard. Even though the tang cavity within the handle will be filled with epoxy, you'll still want to make sure that all of the metal is also coated. This will prevent any moisture from coming into contact with the metal and corroding the exposed surface. Slide the handle material over the tang and tight against the rear of the guard. Fill the cavity with epoxy and move the handle back and forth to ensure all surfaces are thoroughly coated. Smear a little epoxy all over the end of the handle and slip the butt cap over the threaded portion of the tang. Position the butt cap properly, attach the round nut to the tang and tighten (don't over tighten, snug is good enough). Wipe off any excess epoxy with a damp rag and let everything dry overnight.

When the epoxy has dried and hardened, it's time to finish shaping the handle and the butt cap. Wrap the handle in a piece of scrap leather and clamp it in the vise. Using a medium-sized half-round file, bring the butt cap and end of the handle inline with one-another. Cut a slight bevel around the perimeter of the butt cap, and bring the handle down to meet the edge of cap. After the file work is complete, use a strip of cloth-backed abrasive to smooth everything up. Use a 400-grit abrasive, followed by a 600-grit abrasive, to smooth out both the brass butt cap and the guard.

Now that the knife is completed, we'll need a sheath for safe carrying convenience. And that's the subject of the next chapter. You'll note that sharpening the blade is left until last. And this is why most knife makers still have all their fingers. Working with a sharpened blade is outright dangerous. We'll cover this aspect of knife building in an upcoming chapter.

Handle material

Almost anything can be used to cover or enclose a blade tang. However, there are several traditional materials that have been favorites for years. A selection of the most popular handle material choices are listed below:

Bone: Bone knife handle scales are crafted from the shin bone of cattle. Since this material is smooth, it is often jigged or picked to give it texture. Bone can be dyed many different colors and shades. One negative aspect of working with this material is that it smells horrible when ground or filed.

Carbon fiber: This material is made up from tiny strands of carbon, tightly woven together and impregnated with epoxy. It has a three-dimensional look and is both light and extremely rugged. It can be left in a rough state or highly polished.

Corian: Made from various minerals combined with acrylic resin, this material resembles stone. However, it can be worked like any hardwood. Available in many colors and shades, Corian is tough and needs no external finish.

G-10: This material is made from epoxy-impregnated fiberglass. Similar to Micarta in construction, layers of fiberglass material are soaked in resin and subject to heat and pressure. Impervious to most substances, including moisture, this material makes for strong, lightweight knife handle material that can be polished, sandblasted or even checkered.

Horn: Buffalo, sheep and African antelope horn can be used as knife handle material. Horn has a naturally rough or irregular surface that both looks good when polished and offers an excellent hand-to-knife grip surface. To prevent cracking and shrinkage, all horn should be subjected to a stabilization process.

Ivory: Elephant, walrus, mammoth and mastodon ivory have all been used for handle material. They all share the same problem: exorbitant cost. In addition, with the exception of fossilized mammoth and mastodon ivory, it's difficult to obtain elephant and walrus ivory. Ivory is stunning beautiful, especially the fossilized bark (outer layer that has absorbed mineral coloration) ivory from mammoth and mastodon tusks.

Leather: Leather washers, stacked one-on-top-of-another on the blade tang, can be used as a durable and attractive handle material. It is necessary, however, to treat the leather with a preservative to keep it from drying out and shrinking.

Micarta: This material is layers of either linen cloth or paper soaked in phenolic resin and subjected to heat and pressure. The result is an extremely tough material that is available in a wide variety of colors and can be polished or sand-blasted.

Stag: Sections of antler from various deer species can be used, either whole in the round or split into scales, to make very attractive knife handles. Tropical deer, like Sambar and axis, have antlers that are less pithy in the middle than most other species and are the preferred choice of antler material.

Wood: One of the more popular handle material, wood combines beauty and warmth with easy workability. Many types of wood can be used, including both natural and laminates.

Material stabilization

The biggest problem encountered when using wood, horn and other natural materials for knife handles is their tendency to absorb ambient moisture and shrink, warp and crack. With the exception of a few types of wood (desert ironwood, ebony, lignum vitae, etc.), most will benefit from stabilization processing.

Stabilization is a two-part process whereby acrylic resins are infused (forced) into the wood under pressure, followed by a period of curing. An initiator is used to polymerized the liquid resins into a solid form. The result is a product that's resistant to water, oil, stain and dye. Furthermore, stabilized wood is harder than wood in its natural state. And stabilized materials can be machined and drilled, as well as polished without the need for an external finish.

While stabilization doesn't totally prevent wood movement from ambient moisture intrusion, it does provide an enhanced measure of stability to the wood fibers. Should movement occur, it will be much slower and not to the extent of unprocessed wood. Resistance to moisture and some chemicals is increased, and the wood grain will not be affected. Water marking can happen if stabilized wood is soaked, but simple buffing will restore the wood to its original state.

Stabilization imparts several advantages to the knife handle. It enhances the wood grain structure, finish and appearance; protects from environmental invectives; forestalls cracking due to moisture intrusion; and eliminates the need for applying an external finish.

This Trout knife features a Lamb (a noted ergonomic designer) style handle, 3" slender blade and Loveless's Riverside logo.

R.W LOVELESS
maker
Riverside, Calif.

Only one of five similar straight Loveless hunters that feature the dual logo (blade and Ricasso). This particular knife has a 4-3/4" blade and a stag handle.

LOVELESS

R.W. LOVELESS
maker
Riverside, Calif.

A one-of-a-kind stainless knife and fork set with black Micarta handles, made by Loveless.

R. W. Loveless, Knifemaker
P.O. Box 7836
Riverside, Ca. 92503
Shop Phone (714) 689-7800

This well-used Loveless fixed-blade features a brass-wrapped tang and was made for a northern California rancher. According to the documentation provided by Loveless, the knife was used to skin over 3,000 coyotes, as well as deer and other critters.

R.W. LOVELESS
maker
Lawndale, California

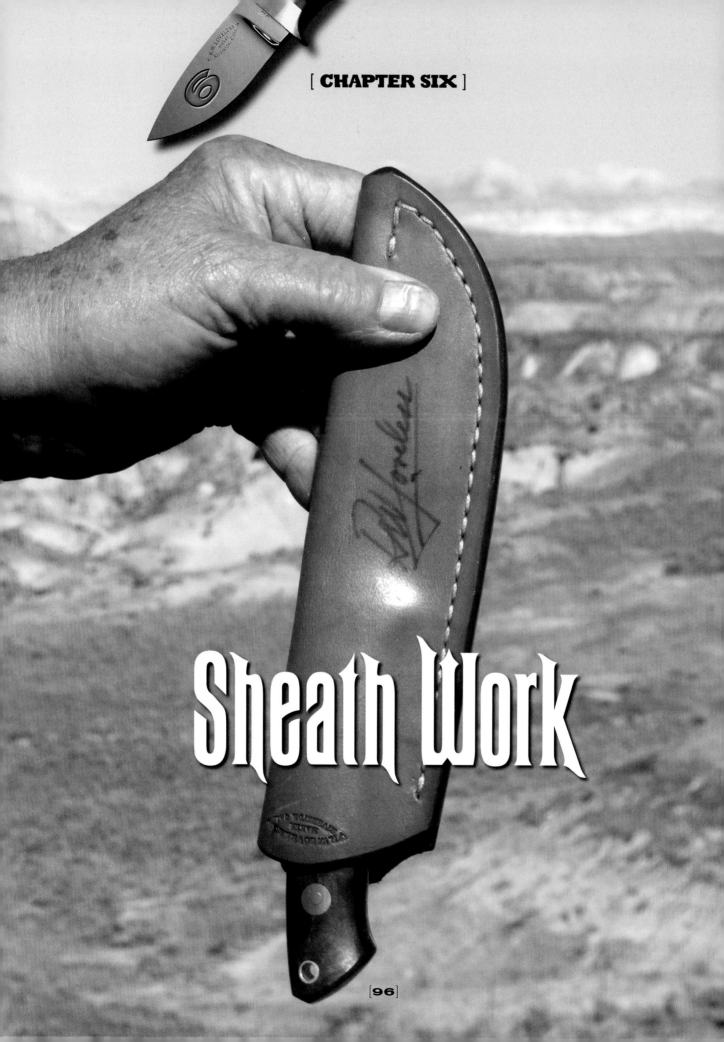

CHAPTER SIX

Sheath Work

A QUALITY KNIFE DESERVES COMPARABLE CARRYING CONTAINMENT, THE LOVELESS POUCH SHEATH PROVIDES SECURITY AND USER SAFETY

A knife sheath is nothing more or less than a transport mechanism. Obviously, the blade edge of a knife is sharp. If that edge is not adequately covered with some type of cut-resistant material, carrying the knife from place to place would pose the risk of accidental injury.

You can bet that whatever material was used to sheath the first edged cutting tools provided a degree of protection for both the tool and tool carrier alike. It's possible that the earliest sheaths were constructed from naturally occurring materials. However, when the science of animal hide preservation was developed, tanned leather became the sheath material of choice.

Leather comes in many grades and weights and the most suitable for knife sheaths isn't inexpensive. Since most knife users don't understand the difference, some knife makers (including production cutlery firms) often get away with using the cheap stuff. I've seen sheaths, even on some rather pricey cutlery, that were little more than "cardboard" leather.

Of course, a leather sheath demands a certain level of care. Over time it can dry out and crack, especially if it's exposed to periods of repeated moisture exposure and heat. And leather can harbor

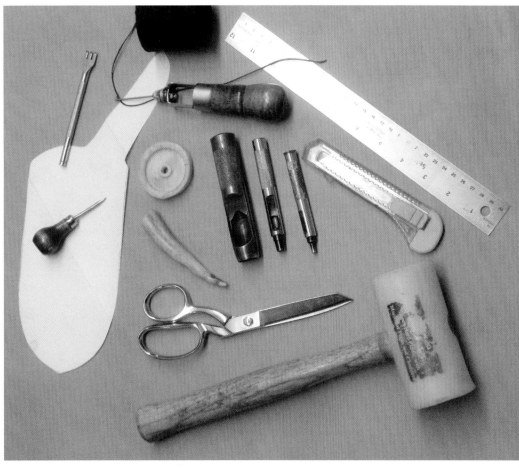

(opposite) When the sheath is finished it should safely hold your knife – even if it's positioned upside-down. (Image: Durwood Hollis)

Making a pouch sheath for your new knife necessitates the acquisition of several leather working tools. Pictured here is such an assortment, including a mallet, punches, sewing awl, waxed nylon thread, scissors, ruler, edging tools and a cutting implement. (Image: Durwood Hollis)

fungus and mold, resulting in rot. The same can be said about any leather product, from saddles to knife sheaths. However, periodic care can easily eliminate most, if not all, of these adverse conditions.

To be sure, a sharp knife can cut through a leather sheath. The purpose of a heavy leather welt along the area where the blade edge rests inside a sheath is to protect the sheath from the sharpened edge. Even so, if the knife isn't carefully placed into the sheath, the blade can cut right through the leather.

Many years ago, I witnessed just such an event. A prospective knife buyer was examining a knife at a local sporting goods establishment. In one hand, he held the sheath and in the other, the knife. When he attempted to insert the knife into sheath, he carelessly shoved the blade right through the body of the sheath and into the palm of his hand. The result was a serious laceration, lots of blood and a trip to the local hospital emergency room. All of this didn't invalidate the design and construction of the sheath. It did, however, speak to the manner in which the knife was handled.

A range of more modern materials, particularly various thermoplastics, have been used as sheath materials. The cost of a molded sheath is far less, in both manufacturing and material costs, than a leather sheath.

However, if you use an inferior grade of leather or plastics, fashion a design that provides only minimal containment and put little effort into sheath construction, the result is a cheap and shoddy appearance. A well-made knife deserves a sheath that reflects the same quality. And you can't do that if your primary concern is the "bottom line." Whatever problems are inherent in leather, it still remains the sheath material of choice of most knife makers. And a quality leather sheath will have nearly as much thought in the design and integrity in the construction as the knife itself.

Regarding knife sheaths, Bob said, "If you're in the market for a new house, you can tell a lot about it by looking at the outside. If the lawn is need of care, the paint on the house faded and shingles are missing from the roof, this is a clue to what can be expected on the inside. The same thing is true when it comes to a knife sheath. A well-made knife should be housed in a sheath that reflects its contents. If not, then approach such an acquistion with extreme caution. A sheath is the house in which the knife resides. Likewise, it says a lot about the resident tenant."

The Bob Loveless knife sheath is as functional in design and clean in appearance as his knives. "Even though some makers add tooling to the outside of their sheaths, other than being purely decorative, it doesn't contribute anything to the sheath. Tooling just makes it a lot easier for moisture to intrude into the surface of the leather, which can promote the growth of mold and fungus," Bob said.

Bob likes a pouch-type sheath, and he abhors keeper straps. My own experience with a press-to-fit sheath has been less than exemplary. I once lost a very nice fixed-blade knife from such a sheath. When upright, the sheath was just fine, but put it on an angle or horizontal and the knife could easily work free. I didn't know that and my lack of knowledge resulted in the loss of the knife. However, a Loveless sheath has a built-in leather cam that holds the knife securely, no matter how the knife is carried. Moreover, the sheath covers not only the blade, but also much of the handle. This provides enhanced protection to the total knife. The Loveless sheath holds the knife, while providing one-hand, ready access.

The reason Bob doesn't like keeper straps is his own experience with this type of sheath construction. He pointed out to me that over time a leather strap can stretch. If the keeper strap isn't attached to the sheath, at some point it can go missing. Should the strap be riveted to the sheath, then the rivet can mar the knife handle. Likewise, a metal snap closure can scratch the handle. And no matter what kind of closure is used on the keeper strap, be it a metal snap or hook-n-loop material, it can come loose in the field. When that happens, the odds of accidental knife loss greatly increase.

The position of the belt loop is another sheath consideration that is often an afterthought. If the sheath rides too low, it has a tendency to flop around. Positioned high on the belt, the handle will dig into your side. Some makers even place the belt loop so the knife is carried horizontally. This means that the knife is always in the way and uncomfortable to carry. The Loveless sheath belt loop is positioned so that only a small portion of the knife rides above the beltline. The belt loop comes off the top of the sheath and is folded over and fastened down to the body of the sheath. The knife is securely attached to the belt and it doesn't flop around or dig into your side.

It's now time to make a sheath to fit our Loveless-style knife. In his own shop, Bob has an entire room devoted to sheath making. "Keeping my leather work separate from knife work keeps dirt, grime and oil away from the leather. Once leather gets filthy or oil stained, you'll have one devil of time getting it clean again. And some stain won't ever come out," Bob said. While the beginning knife maker may not be able to create a special leather work room, you can separate your knife work from your sheath work by creating a separate work space.

Leather work tools

If you're going to make your own knife sheaths, a small investment in leather-working tools is necessary. At a minimum you'll need a cutting implement (swivel knife), a grooving tool, an edger, a stitching marker, a mallet with a rubber or leather head, a hand sewing tool and a spool of waxed nylon thread. While you're at it, purchase a can of leather cement.

Some makers like to decorate their sheaths with tool work. A wide assortment of leather tooling stamps, each producing a particular pattern or design, are available from craft and leather working retail shops. Many knife supply outlets also carry leather working tools.

Leather

Typically, high-quality leather sheaths are crafted from 9- to 10-ounce leather. This can be purchased by the piece, or a full side (the best buy). Most full sides of leather have some degree of blemish (faded brand marks, wire fence cuts and other healed scars) on the outer smooth surface. While blemished leather will be less expensive, most makers want their sheath leather to be blemish-free. You'll pay more for such a hide, but it makes a nicer looking sheath.

There are several different processes used to tan a hide, including chrome tanning (soluble chromium salts, primarily chromium sulfate, are used in the tanning process); vegetable tanning (a vegetable solution, made various tree bark and plants is used to tan the leather); alum tanning (aluminum salts are the primary element in this process); chrome oil tanning (chrome tanned leather is treated with an oil preservative); vegetable chrome re-tanning (chromium salts are used on vegetable tanned leather) and chrome vegetable tanning (chrome tanned leather is re-tanned with a vegetable process).

While almost any of these processes can produce fine leather, sheath leather needs to be free from dis-solved salts (deleterious effect on blade steel). Make sure you inquire with your leather supplier regarding the specific tanning process used in the product.

At a minimum, you'll need a piece of leather approximately 10 inches wide and 20 inches long. If you use a full side for sheath making, you can cut out individual sheath patterns without wasting leather. However, if you purchase leather by the piece, you can expect a certain amount of waste. This is why a full side of leather, even though far more costly than an individual piece, is really your best buy. A beginning knife maker may not want to invest a sizeable sum in a full side, so purchasing leather in smaller pieces may be a better allocation of funds. However, if you plan on making several knives, or want to get into knife making on a regular basis, you'll save money in the long run by purchasing your sheath leather in a larger quantity.

Making a pattern

Since every knife will need its own sheath, your initial assignment will be to draw a sheath pattern on paper that can be transferred onto the leather. Obtain a sheet of heavy craft

The first thing you'll need to do is to make a sheath pattern. Lay your knife down flat on a piece of heavy paper and draw around the perimeter of the knife. Make sure you leave enough room on either side of the knife to fold the pattern over on top of itself. And don't forget to provide for the belt loop. (Image: Durwood Hollis)

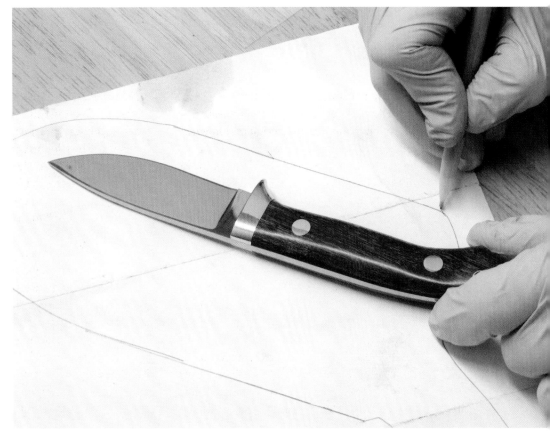

paper or poster paper from your nearest craft store.

Using a straight edge, scribe a centerline down the middle of the pattern paper. This will serve as a control line for the sheath pattern.

Place the knife, edge up point toward you, on this centerline. Ensuring that the back of the knife remains on the centerline, roll it to your right. The edge of the blade should now face away from the centerline. Hold the knife in this position with one hand and with the other draw a line completely around the knife from about one inch below the blade tip to about two inches from the handle butt. Make this line approximately one inch away from the body of the knife. Your initial line can be nothing more

(below) Transfer the pattern to the leather. You'll note that plastic gloves are worn to keep finger prints and grime from marring the smooth side of the leather. (Image: Durwood Hollis)

(right) Using a heavy-duty pair of scissors, cut out the pattern you've drawn on the leather. (Image: Durwood Hollis)

(left) Carefully cut the pattern out and make sure it fits the knife. If it doesn't fit, make another and include the necessary corrections. Adjustments made in the pattern will insure that the finished sheath fits the knife properly. (Image: Durwood Hollis)

than light dashes that mark the outer margin. Afterwards, you can use a ruler to ensure that the final line is correct. This line will serve as the edge of the sheath pattern.

Keeping the back of the knife parallel with the centerline on the paper, roll the knife to the left and repeat the procedure as outlined above. In addition, include a belt loop flap at the top of the sheath pattern. This should be a little more than half the width of one side of the sheath and about half the length. The flap should provide enough space for belts up to two inches in width. When you've finished, check the pattern drawing to make sure it entirely covers the knife.

"When making a pattern for a sheath, you have plenty of opportunity to make corrections. If you check the knife against the pattern, you won't waste a good piece of leather because you failed to correct a mistake early on," Loveless said.

Transferring the pattern

When you're sure that the paper pattern fits right, it's time to transfer it to the leather. Place the pattern on the rough side of the leather, hold it down securely and use a ballpoint pen to trace around the outer margin. When the pattern is removed, you should be able to see it replicated on the leather. If your pen has skipped any place during the transfer, replace the pattern and make the correction. Once you've accurately transferred the pattern to the leather, it's time to start cutting.

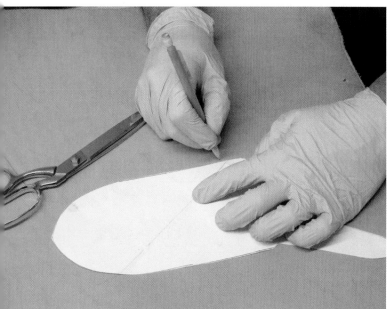

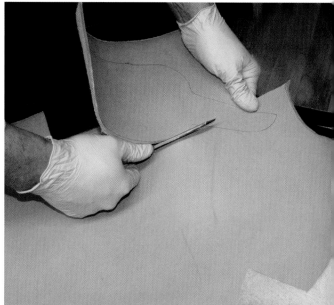

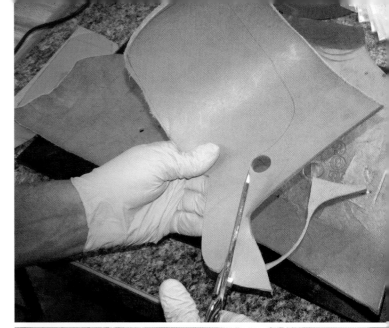

(top) Since it can be difficult to cut tight corners with scissors, a punch has been used for that purpose. (Image: Durwood Hollis)

(middle) Lay the knife down with the spine at the mid-point of the sheath leather. Draw out the position of the welt. Once you've done that, trace the welt pattern onto paper and transfer that pattern to another piece of leather. (Image: Durwood Hollis)

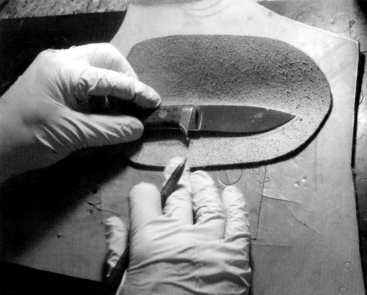

(bottom) Use your scissors to cut out the welt. Set the welt leather aside for attachment later in the project. (Image: Durwood Hollis)

Cutting out the sheath blank

Place the leather on some type of cutting board (a piece of scrap plywood works), and cut out the sheath blank with a swivel knife. If you haven't cut leather before, you'll want to practice first on a scrap piece. Once you feel confident working with the swivel knife, cut out the sheath blank.

Grooving

Next, you'll need to establish a centerline on the rough side of the leather. This line should match the one on the paper pattern. Using the centerline as a guide, position the knife on the sheath blank and mark where the guard comes into contact with the sheath. Lay the knife aside and, with a leather grooving tool, cut shallow grooves on either side of the centerline about 1/8-inch apart. The grooves will allow the leather to fold over smoothly and form the blade containment pocket.

Since you'll want a smooth, rounded fit for the handle, more grooving will have to be done. Make two more shallow grooves, parallel with and about 3/8-inch away from the centerline grooves. Both of these grooves should begin just below the top of the sheath and run to the bottom of the handle. These two grooves will allow the upper portion of the sheath to conform to the rounded shape of the handle.

The next step will be to groove the belt strap so it can also fold easily without cracking the smooth side of the leather. Draw a straight line across the belt strap just above where it joins the body of the sheath. Following this line, use the grooving tool to cut a single shallow groove across the rough side of the belt strap.

While grooving the leather will make it easier to fold, a sheath can be made without this step.

Making the welt

The welt within the sheath not only provides enhanced structural integrity, it also protects the stitching from coming into contact with the blade edge. Lay the

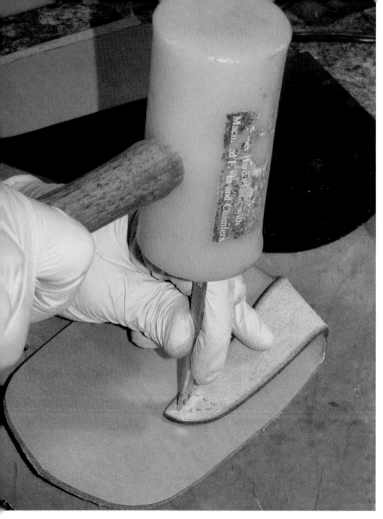

(left) Fold the belt loop over onto the back of the sheath and punch the thread holes. (Image: Durwood Hollis)

(below) Attach the belt loop to the sheath using a simple lock-stitch. (Image: Durwood Hollis)

leather out on a flat surface and, using a ballpoint pen, sketch out the welt piece. Begin sketching at the tip of the knife and make a line that runs the length of the containment pocket of the sheath. This line should match the outline of the knife itself. Instead of a right angle to delineate the guard, make a slight curve. This curve will become a cam of sorts within the containment pocket and prevent the knife from accidentally falling out of the sheath. Draw another line about 3/4 to one inch away from the initial line almost all the way down to the bottom of the sheath.

Next, check the fit of the welt within the sheath. Take your knife and place it into the nearly dry sheath blank, with the back of the knife along the centerline. Position the welt up against the knife facing the outer side of the sheath. Hold the welt in place and fold the opposing side of the sheath blank over until it meets the welt side. Hopefully, everything fits right. If not, now is time to make adjustments. Open the sheath blank and remove the knife. Now, mark the exact position of the welt.

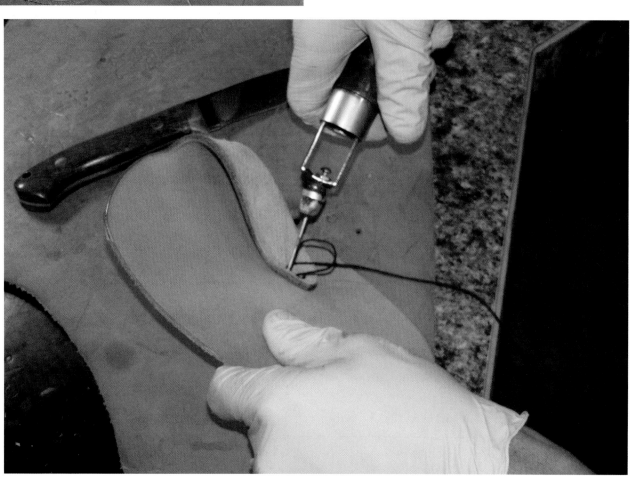

Forming the belt loop

Fold the belt loop over onto the back side of the sheath leather. Make sure you leave a slight gap in the strap for insertion of a belt.

Leather glue or contact cement comes in a small can with a lid-attached brush. Use the brush to carefully lay down a film of glue on the area you've marked for the attachment of the belt strap to the body of the sheath. Stay inside of the perimeter of the marked-off area. Do the same thing on the rough side of the leather strap where it meets the sheath. Let the glue set for a few moments, until it's almost dry to the touch. To expel all of the tiny air pockets from the glued portions, use a mallet and tap the strap down. You can use a hammer, but make sure you place a piece of scrap leather over the area that will come into contact with the hammer. This will ensure that the face of the hammer doesn't mar the smooth leather surface. After the glue has completely dried, the strap can be stitched down by hand (with a lock stitch sewing awl) or riveted. If you don't feel competent with either method, take the sheath to a shoe repair shop and have it stitched in place.

Wet forming

One of the significant properties of leather is that it stretches slightly when wet and can be formed to a particular shape. For the sheath maker, these characteristics are highly desirable. Forming a sheath to an individual knife guarantees secure containment when carried on the belt.

The first step in wet forming is to dampen (not soak) the leather with hot water. Turn on the hot water tap and run the water over both sides of sheath blank until the leather turns a dark color. Fold both sides of the sheath blank together and put the knife into the sheath. Position the knife correctly and press-mold the damp leather against the knife, giving extra attention to the area around the guard and the handle. Also, press the leather against the blade on both sides. What you're attempting to do is imprint the shape of the knife in the leather. After you've adequately wet-formed the leather to conform to the desired shape, remove the knife and wipe it dry. Applying a light film of oil on the blade will prevent rust.

"When you're wet-forming a sheath blank, make sure that your hands are free from oil, dirt and grit. Whatever marks or stains you accidentally get on the smooth side of the leather cannot be removed later. So use care and keep your hands clean," Loveless advises.

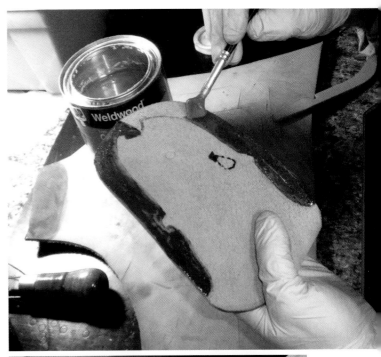

(top) Once you've attached the belt loop, it's time to glue the welt inside of the sheath. Use a small brush and paint the glue onto both sides of the sheath in the area where they will be sewn. (Image: Durwood Hollis)

(above) Paint contact cement onto both sides of the welt leather and place it in position on one side of the sheath. When the welt has been positioned, fold the sheath so that both margins meet. Use your fingers to press down on the leather where the sides meet. (Image: Durwood Hollis)

(above) When both sides are glued together, the sheath should look just like this. (Image: Durwood Hollis)

(right) Take a knife and shave down the glued sheath joint so it's smooth. Afterwards, use a wet sponge or rag and moisten the glued joint. While the leather is damp, use an edging tool to round off the sharp edges. (Image: Durwood Hollis)

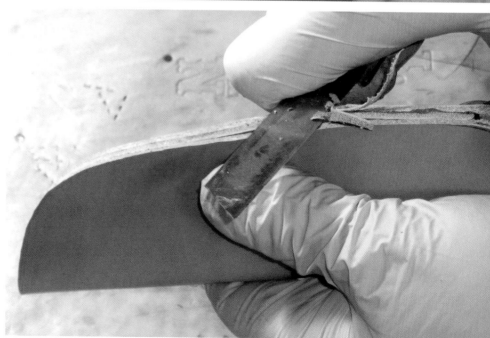

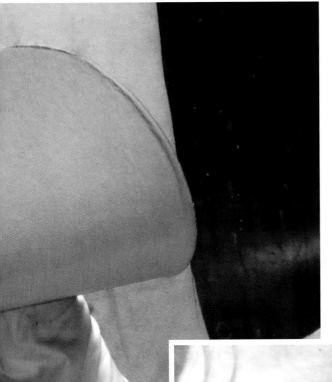

Gluing

Once the welt is properly positioned, it's time to glue it in place. Coat the surface of the welt that matches its appropriate position inside the sheath thoroughly with leather glue. To ensure that the welt is firmly attached, it's best to stitch down the inner margin. Once again, this can be done by hand (tedious) or by machine (your local shoe repair shop).

With the welt in place, it's time to join both sides of the sheath blank. However, Loveless suggests that the fit of the knife within the sheath be checked once again. Place the knife in the sheath, with the back aligned with the centerline. Bring both sides of the sheath blank together to form a containment pouch. Take the knife in and out of the sheath a number of times to check the final fit. If everything works right, proceed with joining the sides of the sheath blank. Using the leather glue, coat the matching surfaces within the sheath blank. Let the

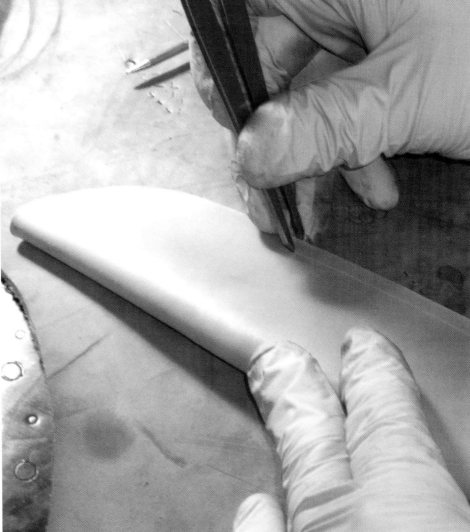

(right) Use a set of calipers to mark the sewing line – 1/4 inch from the edge is about right. (Image: Durwood Hollis)

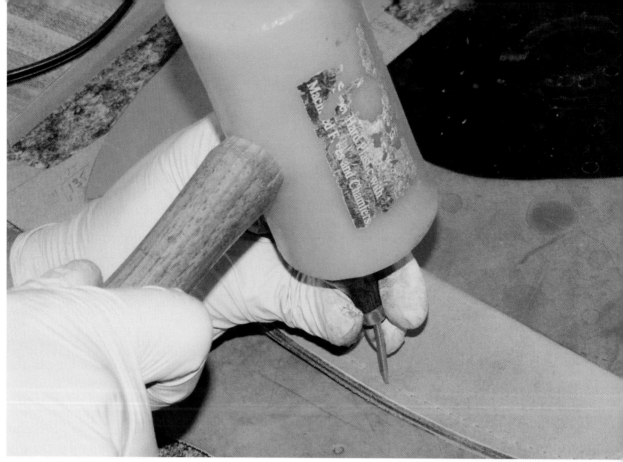

glue set up to nearly dry, then join both halves of the sheath blank together, tapping down the glued joint.

When the glued joint has fully dried, you'll need to stitch the sheath together. Whether the stitching is done by hand or machine, make sure that each stitch is pulled up tight to totally lock the sides of the sheath together in a permanent joint. Finally, use your swivel knife to trim off any extra leather at the edge. What you want to end up with is a border of leather about 1/4 inch beyond the line of stitching. Use a leather edging tool to smooth down all of the sharp edges. The rough edges of the leather should be sanded down smooth and the end of the sheath should be rounded off.

Fit and finish

The final fit of the knife within the sheath is an important step. Wet the sheath once again with hot water. While the leather is damp, work the knife in and out of the sheath several times. As the leather dries, uses hand pressure to mold the sheath to knife. While you're at it, insert your belt into the belt loop and make sure it fits nice and tight. If the belt loop is too tight, it can be stretched a little while the leather is damp. A few slight adjustments now will make a big difference when the leather is completely dry and the sheath ready for service.

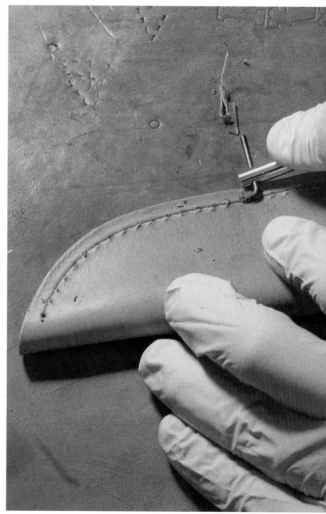

(left) A sewing hole marking tool can be used to indicate the series of holes through which the sheath will be sewn. Once the position of the holes has been marked, use an awl to punch through the leather and create the individual thread holes. (Image: Durwood Hollis)

(bottom left) When the thread holes have been punched, cut a shallow groove to connect each hole. When the sheath is sewn, the groove will keep the thread beneath the surface of the leather. (Image: Durwood Hollis)

(below) Using the sewing awl and waxed nylon thread, sew the border of the sheath with a lock-stitch. (Image: Durwood Hollis)

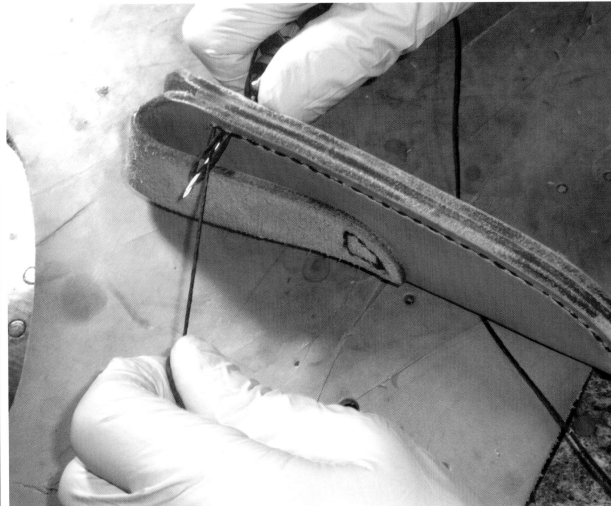

Care and keeping

To finish the sheath, many makers use dye to darken the leather. However, if you simply warm the sheath in the hot sun or use a warm oven (don't overdo the heat because you can damage the leather), the leather will easily soak up a coating of Neatsfoot oil and darken slightly. While neatsfoot oil is an excellent leather conditioner, if you apply too much it can also soften the leather. Use this conditioning oil sparingly. Finally, a coat of leather finishing wax (available at any knife supply firm) will bring out a natural shine. Even neutral shoe polish will work. While your knife sheath should provide outstanding service, exposure to the elements can harm it. An occasional application of conditioner and wax will keep the leather in good shape for years to come.

Neatsfoot Oil

The word "neat" is an old archaic term for animals with hooves (cattle, horses, pigs, etc.). Originally, neatsfoot oil was made from the hooves of these animals. Most of this oil produced today is derived from pig lard, supplemented with mineral oil.

What's next

Over the course of several chapters we've crafted a blade, made a handle and created a sheath. To prevent accidental injury, all of this has been done with an unsharpened blade. Knife sharpening is a process in and of itself. There are many ways to accomplish this assignment and we'll now cover those that produce the best results in the least amount of time. We are now at this juncture in our knife building project. Simply stated, it's time to put the final edge on the blade.

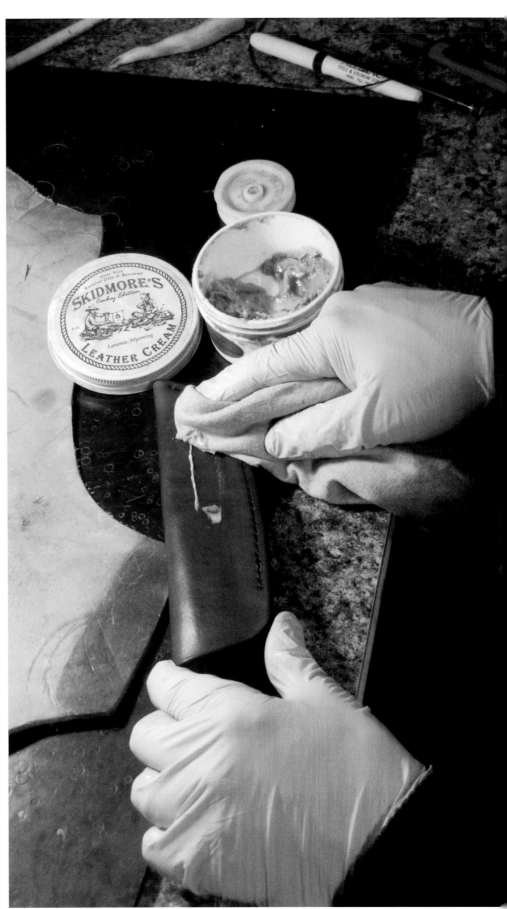

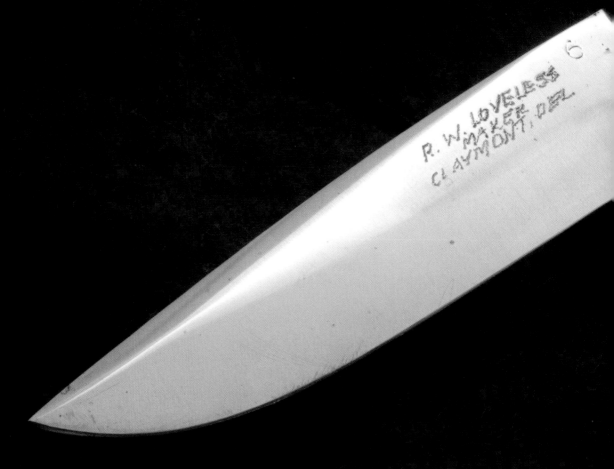

This hunter was produced in 1954, when Loveless
resided in Claymont, Delaware. It features a 4" blade,
brass fittings, leather washer, finger-grooved handle
and aluminum butt.

This clip pattern, Bowie-style fighter with a brass double guard and leather washer handle was made in 1955.

A Loveless/Johnson sub-hilt fighter made on special order for Harry Archer. The knife has a modified clip-pattern blade, stainless fitting and stag handle scales.

LOVELESS maker JOHNSON

WANTED
DELAWARE
by R.W. LOVELESS

MARKED VON LENGERKE
AND ANTOINE CHICAGO

Send D

49
La

CHAPTER SEVEN

Edge Work

EDGE MAINTENANCE
GUARANTEES
PEAK PERFORMANCE

(opposite) This Loveless Bowie-style, clip-point, fixed-blade has lots of edge, all of which needs to be carefully sharpened. Using the right edge establishment and finishing tools, along with appropriate edge geometry, will maximize performance. (Image: Hiro Soga/ John Denton Collection)

(right) Testing the sharpness of a knife edge on the fleshy pad of your thumb is a laceration in the making. (Image: Durwood Hollis)

One of the more challenging assignments for any knife maker is edge establishment. No matter how attractive a knife may be, or how exotic the blade and handle material, if the edge isn't up to par then performance will be negatively impacted.

At a recent knife expo, I looked on as individuals politely asked to examine a particular knife. At some point in that inspection, they always checked the edge for sharpness. Some used the fleshy pad of their thumb (an accident in the making); others used the smooth surface of a finger nail (the better choice). Interestingly, there were knives that apparently didn't past the test. You could tell by how fast the knife was returned to the display table. Obviously, the condition of the edge told the potential buyer all they needed to know.

A better way to test the sharpness of a particular blade is to slide the edge slowly along the surface of a fingernail. Since the nail is as smooth as glass, if the blade has been honed properly, it will hang up on the surface.
(Image: Durwood Hollis)

Whether you use a knife regularly or only on occasion, having a sharp edge is paramount. While most knife makers understand this and do their best to provide edge integrity in every one of their products, they don't always impart that knowledge to those who purchase their knives. Absent adequate blade edge maintenance information, the knife will likely be used beyond acceptable performance parameters.

A friend of mine is so challenged by knife sharpening that he has abandoned any attempt to succeed in that endeavor. However, he always seems to arrive in hunting camp with a sharp knife. His solution to the dogged demand of edge maintenance is to purchase a new knife every time he goes on a hunt. Since he buys the same knife model, no one is the wiser and his problem is solved. Even though I've tried to teach him about edge maintenance, he replies by telling me that "a new knife is better than trying to gain knowledge of a skill set that seems impossible to learn."

Edge angle

It wasn't necessarily a new knife that I needed. On a hunt many years ago, any knife would have been welcome. You see, I'd somehow forgotten to pack a knife with my hunting gear. When I arrived at the ranch where the hunt was to occur, the hour was late and the nearest town was about 40 miles away. Knifeless, alone and left with no other alternative, I rummaged through every cupboard and drawer in the tiny cabin kitchen looking for some type of edged tool. Finally, I discovered a paring knife of dubious age and construction.

Of course, the knife was dull and the edge was badly

chipped, but a little whetstone work could fix that. Unfortunately, my whetstone was at home with my knife. However, there was a concrete step outside of the cabin door that could serve as an abrasive surface. With a splash of soapy water for lubricant, the right sharpening angle and a serious expenditure of effort, I was able to produce an almost adequate edge on that little knife. A folded and duct-taped piece of cardboard served as a sheath and I was "good to go." Before the hunt was over, I used that knife to field-dress and skin a bull elk.

This illustration shows that the knife, the sharpening medium or even the sharpening technique aren't the most important elements in this paradigm. What is important, however, is the angle in which the blade edge is presented to the abrasive surface. The consistent nature of that presentation is also a component in the process.

The late author Peter Hathaway Capstick once told me over lunch near his home in South Africa that, "A proper blade edge is two corresponding angles, meeting at infinity."

Indeed, when a knife blade has been keenly honed it will focus its cutting energy at the apex of the paired edge angles. When that apex becomes abraded through usage, the paired edge angles no longer meet at "infinity." This being the case, the cutting edge has become many times wider than it was when originally sharp. Having lost its integrity, the force necessary for the edge to overcome resistance is also multiplied exponentially, making the movement of the blade through a cutting medium totally unpredictable. This unpredictable nature of a dull knife creates the potential for injury.

At one time or another, all of us have or will push the limits of cutting edge performance. My own experience in this realm came on a long ago deer hunt. In the area where the hunt occurred, you're allowed to take two bucks. As luck would have it, I was able to fill both of my deer tags on the first day of the hunt. After field-dressing, skinning and

de-boning all of the meat, I decided to cut the venison into steaks and roasts. About halfway through that chore, I noticed that my knife edge was dragging just a bit. Obviously, it was time to stop and put a few calories into edge restoration, but stubbornly I pushed on.

Each cut became more and more difficult, demanding increased pressure on the blade to achieve the desired effect. Then it happened: I lacerated the thumb on my opposing hand, nearly down to the bone. It wasn't a simple adhesive bandage repair; it was an 80-mile roundtrip to the nearest emergency room and multiple sutures in my hide. When it was all over, my thumb looked like it had come out second best in a bout with a sewing machine. It was tough way to learn how dangerous a dull knife can be.

Edge establishment

Most knife makers use their belt grinder to sharpen their knives, putting the final touch to the edge with stone abrasion. This is a critical step

It's possible to establish a potential edge with nothing more than a small whetstone. However, expect to put serious calories into the assignment. (Image: Durwood Hollis)

in knife making, and a slack belt is generally employed. In some instances, makers have been known to use the disk sanding attachment on an electric drill for the same purpose. However, those who are building their very first knife may not own a belt grinder or an electric drill and all of the edge work will have to be accomplished by hand.

When you began working on the blade blank, you filed a 45-degree angle on either side of the eventual edge zone. While that particular angle might work on a cold chisel, it isn't best cutting edge for a knife blade. Depending on the type of blade steel and its optimal hardness, most makers employ an 18- to 22-degree edge angle. I split the difference and employ a 20-degree angle.

If you're using a belt grinder, always grind with the edge up. This allows you see the progression of your work. It's not necessary to use a new abrasive belt, because it can take off too much metal too quickly. In fact, a belt with a little wear on it is a better option because the work will go slower. However, don't use excessive pressure, because the build-up of heat from pressure will have an adverse effect on steel. This is why a slack belt is generally the best belt grinder sharpening option.

When it comes to the final buffing of the blade edge, don't buff with the cutting edge up. Buff with the edge down, so the buffing wheel won't have anything to grab onto. Because the buffing wheel is soft, you'll tend to put pressure on the blade and it can easily get snatched up, spun around and thrown into you. It happened to me once and the knife ended bouncing off of my foot. That experience made me realize how important it is to wear steel toe footwear when building a knife.

Those who are without a belt grinder will have to use something else to thin the edge zone by hand. For many makers, the tool of choice is whetstone. The whetstone approach takes considerable time. And you'll need solid eye-hand coordination to maintain a consistent sharpening angle. Those who are practiced at the art of whetstone work seem to have no problem establishing a workable edge zone. However, others may experience considerable frustration with this approach. Since you'll want to establish a workable edge zone, begin by using a soft (coarse) whetstone.

Stone abrasion

There are many kinds of whetstones, both natural (silica quartz crystal, known as novaculite) and man-made. These stones come in a variety of shapes (round, flat and triangular) and abrasive grit sizes. Typically, a soft whetstone has extremely large abrasive grain, while a hard stone possesses very fine grain grit. If you're go-

Novaculite

The word "novaculite" comes from the Latin word novacula, meaning razor stone. This material is a type of microcrystalline or cryptocrystalline quartz, which is also recognized as a re-crystallized form of chert. Formed in the Mississippian and Devonian Period (405 to 350 million years ago), novaculite is a highly siliceous sediment that may have been the product of metamorphism of what was originally beds of chert.

Typically, this material is a hard, very dense, white-to-grayish black sedimentary rock. The tiny crystalline points (nodules) are quite similar to diamonds in hardness, but are less abrasive and possess better polishing qualities. While there may only be minor differences in the size of the grain from one grade of stone to another, the abrasive quality of each is directly related to the density or compact nature of the individual bladed quartz crystals that make-up the novaculite.

Whetstone can come in many colors. During the process of sedimentation that has occurred over the millennia, various trace minerals were also deposited in the stone which accounts for the variation in color. Therefore, color isn't the determining factor in grading novaculite.

The different grades (grit size) of novaculite have differences in texture. Soft stones are rather coarse and harder stones have a progressively smooth or even glassy feel to their surface. After some use, the texture of any whetstone will have a slight amount of change as it goes through a breaking-in period.

This material was first used by American aboriginals who produce cutting tools and weapons from novaculite. Trading between the various tribal groups resulted in the use of this stone being spread far and wide throughout the North American continent.

The largest deposit of novaculite is found in the Quachita Mountains of Arkansas.

Several firms have mineral and mining rights in this area and each has their own quarry where the stone is mined and cut. In some instances, family-owned Novaculite quarries can be dated to the 1800s.

ing to use stone abrasion for edge establishment, then a soft (coarse) whetstone is the starting point to thin the edge, followed by a medium, and then a hard (fine) stone, respectively.

Whetstone sharpening is accomplished by repeatedly stroking the blade edge across the abrasive surface, alternating sides on each pass. Since you'll have to thin the edge down, expect to put some effort into the task. The appropriate edge-to-abrasive angle cannot be emphasized enough. If the angle isn't consistently replicated, then you won't make any progress. And therein lays the difficulty of freehand sharpening.

I've watch several of my friends attempt to sharpen their knives on a whetstone, only to see the whole pro-

(left) To use a whetstone for edge establishment, as well as final finishing, you must choose the right abrasive, set an appropriate blade-to-abrasive angle (18 to 22 degrees) and pass the edge over the stone in a consistent manner.

(below) Edge zone establishment and sharpening is accomplished by moving the blade edge across the whetstone, alternating sides on every pass. The key to this work is replicating the identical edge angle each and every time the blade is in contact with the abrasive surface. (Image: Durwood Hollis)

Whetstone work will produce results according to the amount of effort you put into the task, as well as the technique employed. Either light oil or water will keep the stone free from metal fines and allow the abrasive to do its job.
(Image: Durwood Hollis)

cedure end up in frustration. The primary principle of whetstone use is the establishment and maintenance of the same edge-to-abrasive angle throughout the sharpening procedure. Quite frankly, that takes solid eye-hand coordination, lot of practice and considerable patience.

Adding to the difficulty of maintaining a consistent angle is that fact that, after repeated usage, the whetstone sharpening bed will become eroded (dished-out). This will affect the edge-to-abrasive angle. As the blade edge passes over the sharpening bed, the sharpening angle can change because the whetstone no longer has a perfectly flat abrasive surface. When this occurs, it's difficult to maintain the proper angle by freehand sharpening.

In addition to natural whetstones, there are manmade alternatives. Basically, these are chemically bonded abrasives (ceramic, diamond and silicon-carbide). They abrade faster and polish less than the natural product. Typically, they are usually more affordable than a natural novaculite whetstone. Since both natural and manmade whetstones come in a variety of configurations and abrasive grit (extremely fine to very coarse), depending on the type and hardness of the blade steel, you may need to use several different stones.

Whetstones are simple to use and will produce results that are directly proportionate to the sharpening technique used and effort expended. Most folks use some kind of honing oil or water to eliminate clogging the pores of the stone. Others prefer to sharpen on a dry stone. I've used both methods and don't really have a preference. Oil can be messy, and a little water seems to work just as well in most instances. And there's nothing wrong with using a dry stone, as long as you first scrub it clean with a stiff brush. This will remove the microscopic fines left behind during the sharpening process.

In Africa after a successful Cape buffalo hunt, I watched several of the men who were gutting and skinning the animal sharpen their knives on nothing more than a flat, smooth rock that had been picked up from a nearby dry riverbed. Those dealing with the buffalo used carbon steel clasp knives. The steel in those knives was relatively soft and it only took a little work with the makeshift rock sharpener to restore an acceptable level of sharpness to the edge. Because every one of those men had worked on countless animals throughout their lives, knife sharpening was a skill that each had learned and perfected over time. And the only lubricant they used on that rock was a little spit. Again, the right sharpening angle is more important than the type of sharpener or lubricant used.

If you're going to use stone abrasion to thin and sharpen the blade edge, here are a couple of tips. Instead of stroking the whetstone (the farther away from your point of origin, the more likely that the edge angle will shift), try moving the blade in tiny circles down the length of the cutting edge. It's a lot easier to maintain the proper angle when you hold the knife close, rather than at arms length.

A clamp-on edge angle guide can ensure the correct presentation of the blade edge to the abrasive surface. Once clamped in place, the guide keeps the edge at a consistent angle no matter what sharpening technique is utilized. In my experience, even a beginner using a clamp-on angle guide can put an edge on a blade quicker than someone with years of freehand sharpening under their belt.

Whetstone alternative

Seeking a better and faster method of edge establishment, some manufacturers have produced a type of whetstone that isn't stone at all. A flat, perforated nickel plate (softer than blade steel) is fused with monocrystalline diamond particles, producing extremely rapid results. As the blade edge is passed over the abrasive surface, the microscopic fines (ground-off metal) are deposited in the openings within the perforated nickel base plate, which prevents the abrasive surface from getting clogged.

This type of sharpener is used just like a traditional whetstone. To initiate sharpening, push the blade away from you like you're attempting to take a thin slice off of the sharp-

As a whetstone alternative, many favor a perforated nickel plate with embedded diamond grit. The holes in the base plate catch the metal fines that are abraded from the edge and keep the diamond abrasive surface clean. (Image: Durwood Hollis)

ening bed. To sharpen the opposite side of the blade, place the blade edge on the opposite end of the sharpener and pull the blade toward you. The user need only set the desired sharpening angle and maintain it during the sharpening process to produce a keen edge. Continue this procedure until you obtain the desired level of sharpness.

Expect a break-in period with this type of sharpener. Initially, the speed at which metal is removed from the edge will be quite aggressive. However, after several uses, you'll notice that the process slows down. This is normal. The diamond surface isn't wearing out. It's just breaking in.

To clean the sharpener, use some kitchen cleaner, water and a stiff brush to remove the leftover fines from the sharpening surface. In addition to the speed at which this type of sharpener produces an edge, there's never a worry about the flatness of the sharpening bed getting worn down over time.

Pre-angled carbide tips

Another quick method of thinning out the edge zone on your new knife is with a tool that many refer to as a "drag-and-scrape" sharpener. This sharpener features a pair of extremely hard tungsten-carbide tips set into a hand tool. The tips are pre-angled, so you don't have to worry about blade edge to abrasive contact.

To use the tool, place it on a flat, sturdy surface. Hold

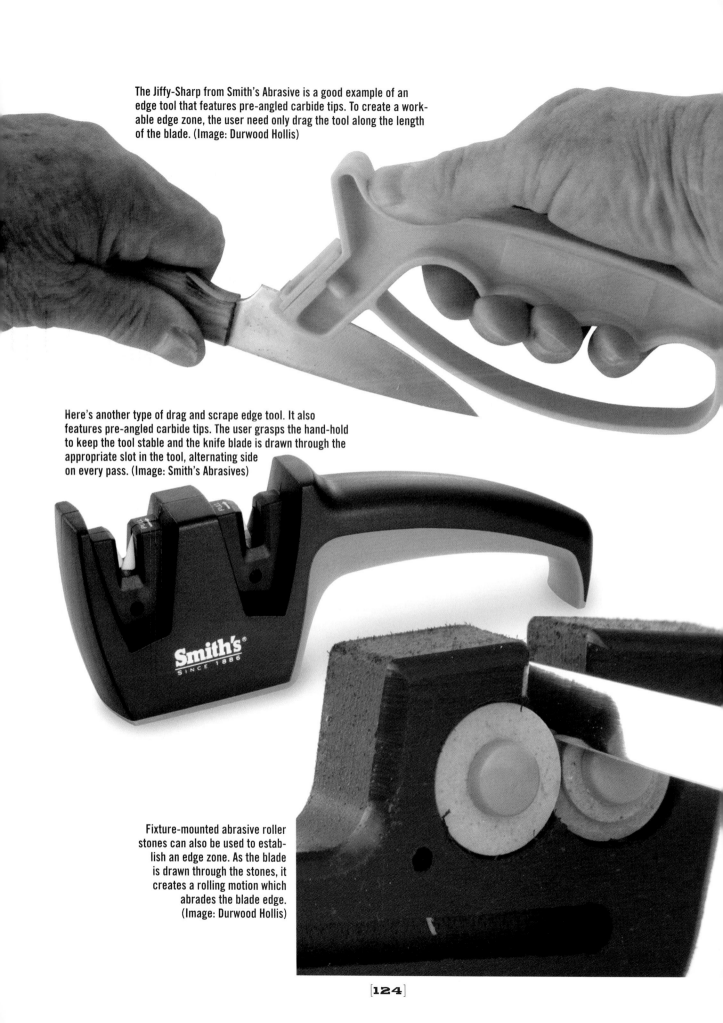

The Jiffy-Sharp from Smith's Abrasive is a good example of an edge tool that features pre-angled carbide tips. To create a workable edge zone, the user need only drag the tool along the length of the blade. (Image: Durwood Hollis)

Here's another type of drag and scrape edge tool. It also features pre-angled carbide tips. The user grasps the hand-hold to keep the tool stable and the knife blade is drawn through the appropriate slot in the tool, alternating side on every pass. (Image: Smith's Abrasives)

Fixture-mounted abrasive roller stones can also be used to establish an edge zone. As the blade is drawn through the stones, it creates a rolling motion which abrades the blade edge. (Image: Durwood Hollis)

the sharpener with one hand for stability and control during the sharpening procedure. Place that portion of the blade edge nearest the guard in the opening between the carbide tips, at 90-degree angle to the tool. Next, exerting slight downward pressure, pull the blade (never back and forth) through the crossed carbide tips, from heel to tip. After a few passes of the blade across the carbide tips, you'll begin to notice a change in the edge geometry as the tool actually peels off metal rather rapidly. When you get the edge zone thinned out to an appropriate angle, then it's time to switch to another type of abrasive to smooth and polish the edge.

A "drag and scrape" alternative uses a set of rolling abrasive stones or disks set in a hand-held fixture. One hand is used to hold the fixture, while the other hand draws the blade through the juncture of the abrasives. The movement of the blade causes the stones to roll on their axis, which in turn abrades an appropriate edge angle on both sides of the blade simultaneously. Some models even include a second set of abrasives in the sharpener to provide a final polish to the edge.

Edge angle fixture tools

This type of sharpener is comprised of a two-piece horizontal clamp, which holds the knife blade. The ends of the horizontal clamp have been bent at right angles and each contains a series of slots that are marked according to the angle they represent.

To use the tool, the knife blade is placed into the horizontal clamp with the edge facing away from the tool. The abrasive material (stone, ceramic, diamond, etc.) is mounted in such a way that each has a long rod sticking out of one end. The rod is inserted into the desire angle slot and the user simply strokes the blade edge to sharpen. When one side of the blade has been sharpened, simply turn the sharpener over, insert the abrasive extension rod in the appropriate slot and repeat the sharpening process. While all of this may sound a bit complicated, it really isn't. And the entire sharpening system is packaged in a self-contained carrying kit.

So-called "V" sharpeners are another edge establishment and maintenance tool that fits into this category. This type of tool also features fixture-mounted edge abrasives. The fixture consists of a molded thermoplastic or wood base with pre-angled openings into which the abrasive material is fitted. The openings in the base correspond to a particular edge angle. The name "V" sharpener comes from the position of the abrasive rods (some

While the edge angle tool requires some assembly, you have a choice of multiple types of abrasives (stone, diamond, ceramic) and the entire unit is fully kit-contained. (Photo: GATCO)

may be triangular) when mounted in the base.

To put this type of tool into action, the user holds the knife blade vertically, which engages the abrasive at an appropriate edge angle, then moves the blade downward and inward at the same time, alternating strokes between the two abrasives. Typically, a pair of diamond abrasives are used to establish the edge zone, followed by a pair of ceramic abrasives to smooth and polish the edge. These units are also self-contained, with the abrasives stored within the base. Other than scrubbing the ceramic abrasives clean with powder kitchen cleaner, upkeep of this type of tool is very minimal.

Electric sharpeners

Any time electric power is added to a blade edge establishment and sharpening tool, much of the drudgery of sharpening is eliminated. This is certainly the reason most professionals use an electric belt grinder with a slack belt to initially establish a blade edge zone. The main problem with power is the spced at which the abrasive is operated. This creates heat and that heat has a negative effect on edge hardness. Of course, the same critical issue remains as with any sharpening system: the appropriate blade edge-to-abrasive angle.

Fortunately, a few innovative manufacturers have solved both the heat build-up and edge angle problems in their electrically-powered sharpeners. The abrasive used is most often diamond, which produces amazingly fast results. Furthermore, the abrasive is embedded into flexible disks that eliminate constant contact with the blade at the same position throughout the sharpening cycle. This also reduces heat-build up.

The edge angle problem is solved by providing several pre-angled sharpening slots in the tool, which correspond to the degree of edge establishment or maintenance needed. One model even incorporates both electrical and manual sharpening elements, which allows the user to set the edge manually with pre-angled carbide tips, and then utilize electrically-powered diamond and ceramic abrasives for the final edge work. I've used these tools for edge zone creation, as well as smoothing and polishing the final edge, and nothing does the job any better or faster.

This electric edge tool by Chef's Choice features three different abrasive slots, from extremely coarse (edge establishment) to extra fine (edge polishing). This type of tool takes much of the drudgery out of edge work.
(Image: Durwood Hollis)

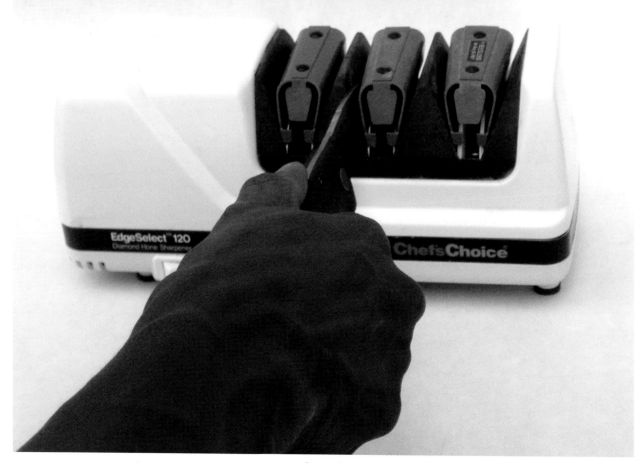

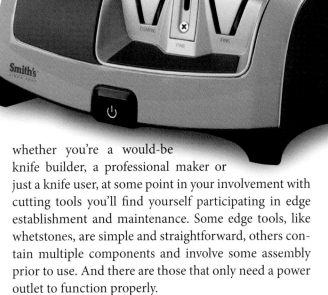

Another electric edge tool is manufactured by Smith's Abrasives. It features the ability to manually set the edge with carbide tips and perform edge finishing and polishing with electrically driven diamond abrasive. (Image: Smith's Abrasives)

Personal preference

Like many hobbyist knife builders, I don't have a huge inventory of tools, including a belt grinder. However, establishing an edge zone and sharpening a knife on a belt grinder is just as challenging as doing it on a whetstone. Therefore, my approach to this assignment is to initially use pre-angled carbide tips to scrape out the primary edge zone. This way there's no problem setting the right angle. When the carbide tips quit peeling off metal, then I switch over to a multi-stage electrically-powered sharpener. As I take the blade through the basic three sharpening steps (coarse, medium and fine), each abrasive slot in the tool smoothes and polishes the edge at an appropriate angle.

It's important to remember there's no do-it-all edge tool for every situation. What you might use for edge zone establishment can be far different from what's used to put the final edge on your blade. The same is true with abrasives. For example: a diamond abrasive might work quickly, but it can leave a visible scratch pattern behind. Depending on the type of final blade finish, you may have to use a series of abrasives to achieve your goal.

There is a host of edge maintenance tools available and every one works more or less effectively. No matter whether you're a would-be knife builder, a professional maker or just a knife user, at some point in your involvement with cutting tools you'll find yourself participating in edge establishment and maintenance. Some edge tools, like whetstones, are simple and straightforward, others contain multiple components and involve some assembly prior to use. And there are those that only need a power outlet to function properly.

In recent years, knife users seem to prefer blade steels that offer enhanced edge retention over sharpening ease. In response, sharpening technology has evolved to deal with edge maintenance more effectively. While a smooth rock may be able to serve as a whetstone, it won't do the job as efficiently as the newer generation of knife sharpening tools. It's as simple as that.

This large ceramic rod has been used by the author for years to put the final edge on many of his knives. Even though ceramic can work as well as other abrasives, the necessity of maintaining and replicating an appropriate edge angle remains. (Image: Durwood Hollis)

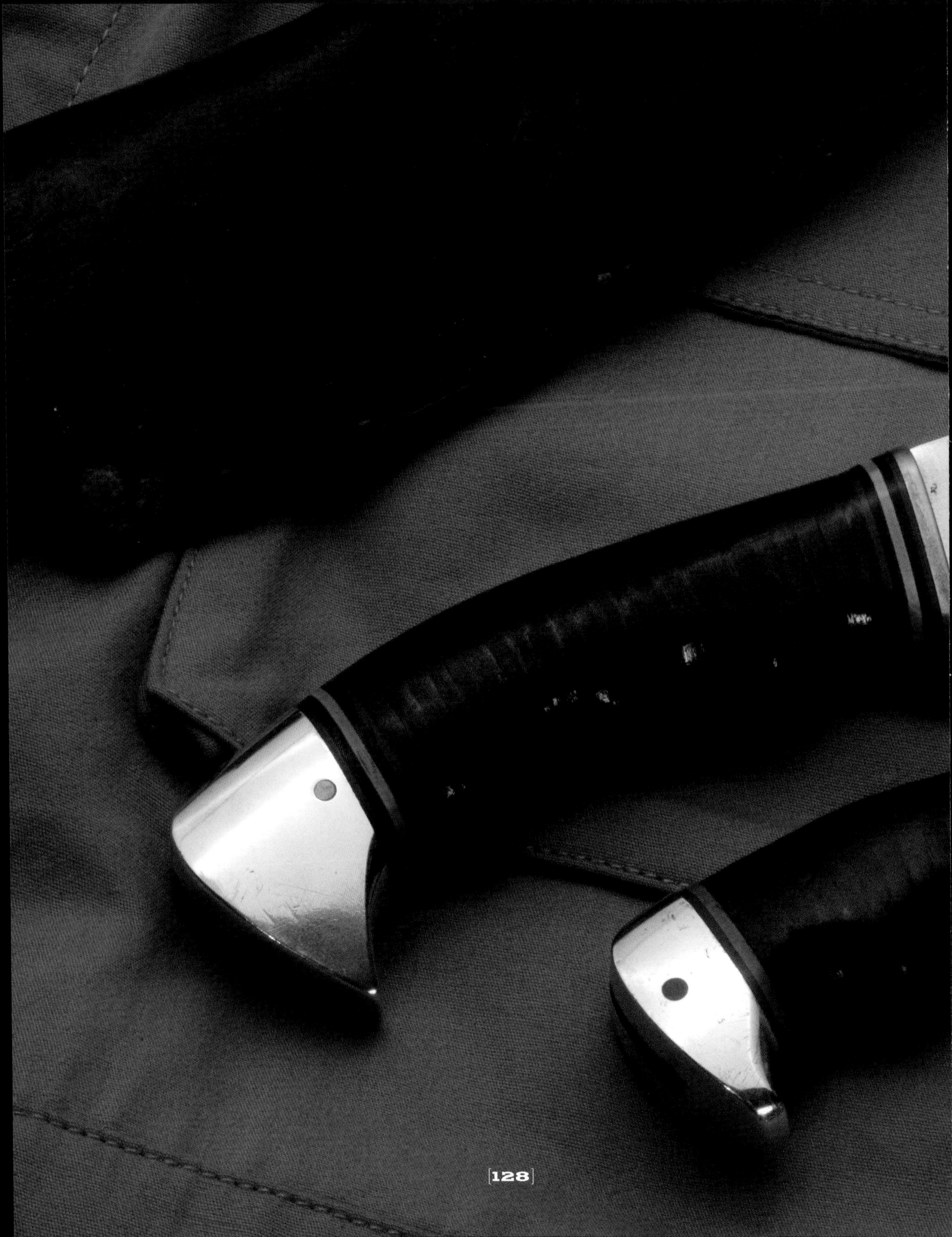

These two early (1956) Loveless fixed blades were made for Abercrombie & Fitch in New York City. Both knives feature carbon steel blades, finger grooved leather washer handles and aluminum butts.

This special fighting knife was produced in Lawndale, California. The knife has a 6-1/2" blade, tulip wood handle and a skull cracker pommel. When Loveless made this knife, he commented that the tulip wood was "the prettiest handle material" he'd ever put on a knife.

A. R.W. LOVELESS
maker
Lawndale, California ▲

Another early (1950s) hunter made by Loveless in Claymont, Delaware. Interestingly, there appear to be thumb notches on the back of the blade, just ahead of the guard. This is an extremely uncommon feature on a Loveless knife.

CHAPTER EIGHT

Knife Care and Keeping

PROPER USE AND CARE PROTECTS YOUR KNIFE AND ITS SHEATH

Everything has use parameters, and when something is used outside of its predetermined role, there are consequences. With a knife, misuse can result in damage to the knife, your person or both.

While antelope hunting with a companion some years ago, just such an event transpired. Even though my friend was an enthusiastic hunter, his experience was limited to a few forays afield years ago with his father. Now a grown man, he had taken up hunting once again. As luck would have it, on this trip he was the first to score on a buck.

When we approached the downed pronghorn, I hung back to see how he was going to handle field dressing. First, he unloaded his rifle and set it aside. Next, he validated his antelope tag. So far, he had taken all of the

(opposite) Both of these Loveless knives have been damaged by misuse. The knife on the left has been reground, but is barely serviceable. The knife on the right, with its tip broken off, is beyond repair. (Image: John Denton)

(below) The Knife & Tool Care Kit from Sentry Solutions has easy-to-use cleaning tools, lubricants, an oil impregnated wiping cloth and even a ceramic sharpener, all contained in a handy, durable nylon pouch. (Image: Durwood Hollis)

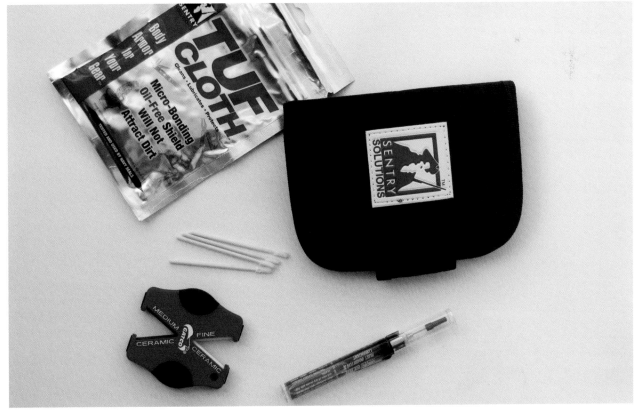

right steps to be safe and legal. That's when things began to go wrong.

He took out his knife, turned toward me, smiled and pointing towards the antelope, and said, "I got this."

Not one to stand in another man's way, I just watched as he began to field dress the animal. He had no problem opening the abdominal cavity, but seemed to stall at the ribcage. As he cut through the cartilage that held the ribs together, I saw him working the handle of his knife back and forth. Even though he obviously stressed the blade, the knife held up and he managed to open the pronghorn from one end to the other. At this point, things seemed to be going well. He hadn't approached the task the same way I would, but I knew better than to interfere.

His next action gave me a bit of concern. He cut through the pelvic area, down to the bone, and removed the animal's genitalia. Next, he inserted the point of his knife into the pelvic suture (the point at which either side of the pelvis is fused together). With considerable force, he began rocking the knife from side to side. I knew this was a problem in the making. Sure enough,

the tip of his knife blade broke and my friend fell on his backside.

Looking at his knife with amazement, he said, "They must not make knives as good as they did when I was a kid."

Of course, knife integrity wasn't the problem. The blade tip broke because of misuse. A knife is designed to cut, and using it as a tool to pry open the pelvic suture is definitely outside of that parameter. If my friend felt the need to cut through the pelvis, a bone saw or even a hand-axe would have been a better tool for the chore.

While it's possible to break through an antelope or deer's pelvis with a knife, it's most certainly not a primary field care necessity. Access to the lower intestinal tract can be made by cutting the anus free and pulling the intestines and bladder up and out of the initial incision in the abdomen. It also wasn't necessary to open the ribcage. An incision through the diaphragm

If used to pry open bone sutures or perform similar activities during field dressing big game, even the best knife can suffer damage. A knife is a cutting tool and that only. (Image: Durwood Hollis)

provides plenty of access to the heart and lungs, without cutting through the ribs.

When I explained all of this to my friend, he nodded his head in agreement. However, when he took another antelope the following season, he started to repeat his disastrous knife use from the previous year. At that point, I stepped in and handed him a bone saw. There was no use trying to change his field dressing mind set, but I could provide the a better tool for the job.

Knife misuse isn't unusual. Quite frankly, it's commonplace. Once, when visiting a production cutlery factory, the owner showed me a box full of knife returns. Without exception, every single knife had a broken blade tip. Those knives had failed not because of inferior manufacturing, but because of misuse. I was even shown a sampling of letters that had accompanied each returned knife, claiming that the knife broke under "normal" circumstances.

When I asked the factory owner how he handled the returned knives, his answer was straightforward, "We just send them a new knife, no questions asked. I want every customer to know that we stand by our knives, no matter what. Our cost to replace a damaged knife is nothing in comparison to the relationship with the customer that's created when he receives a new knife in return," he said. Certainly, the cutlery factory owner's actions were commendable, even though it was clear that every returned knife had been misused.

My father was a knife misuser. He carried a multi-bladed pocketknife that he used for everything from game care to fishing reel repair and a whole lot more. In time, the tips of each of the smaller blades were broken. Not to be deterred, Dad would take the knife out to the garage and use a wheel grinder to square off the blade tip. Once ground square, the blades made passable screwdrivers for slotted screws (the same kind that held his fishing reel together). "Field modifications" he called them. Of course, a small screwdriver would have been better suited for reel repair, but dad only had a pocketknife with him and he used it. Or more precisely, he misused it.

A knife is a knife, not a pry bar, bone saw or screwdriver. Use your knife as it should be used and you most likely won't ever have a problem. Remember that any tool, from a hammer to a chain saw, when used improperly can become a dangerous implement. This is certainly true with a knife.

Now that that we've discussed knife use, let's move on to knife care. Basically, there are two kinds of knives – fixed-blade and folding. The former has no moving parts, therefore it takes less maintenance. The latter,

however, possesses components that move, which necessitates an enhanced level of care.

Fixed-blade knives

Whether carried as an everyday cutting implement or used as a primary field tool, a knife needs to be kept free from dirt, debris, moisture and the fluid byproducts of game care. When it comes to a fixed-blade design, this is not a complex assignment. After use, simply wipe the blade, guard and handle clean and return the knife to the sheath. At

Even if you've wiped your fixed-blade knife in the field, upon returning to camp or home a more thorough cleaning is required. Run hot water over the blade and use a stiff brush to remove any residual blood, fat or grime. (Image: Durwood Hollis)

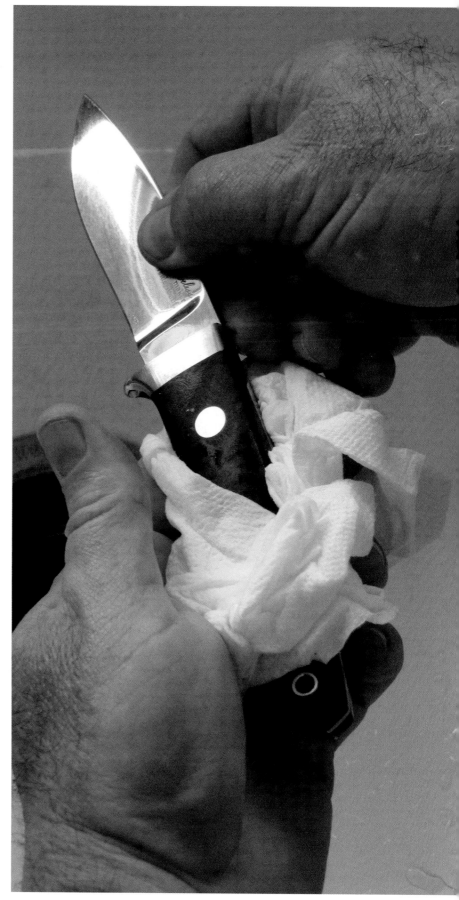

After washing the knife, use a dry towel to wipe it dry. Pay special attention to the area near the guard. (Image: Durwood Hollis)

first glance, one would think that's all there is to it. However, even after an initial cleaning, all kinds of contaminants can hide on a fixed-blade knife, even one with a mirror-polished blade.

While a wash-off and a wipe-down in the field is the first step, a subsequent more thorough cleaning is required to ensure that the corrosive effects of environmental invectives are held at bay. When you return to camp or home, whichever comes first, subject your knife to a more intense cleaning regimen.

Remove the knife from the sheath and set the sheath aside. Use hot water and a small brush (an old tooth brush will work, but a copper or brass brush generally has longer bristles) to scrub the blade and guard, paying particular attention to the joint where the guard adjoins the blade. Hot water not only frees up dried blood and other sticky substances, it also elevates the temperature of the metal. When the knife is dried, the warm metal will cause any remaining moisture to evaporate.

Cleaning a fixed-blade knife handle may take a different approach. Hot water could be detrimental to some wood handle materials. Likewise, hot water isn't recommended for use on stag. The use of a slightly damp (room temperature water), stiff nylon brush won't harm either wood or stag. Afterwards, wipe off any excess moisture and use a hair drier to blow-dry the surface of the handle.

When the knife is clean and dry, coat the blade and any exposed portion of the tang with a film of oil. When it comes to a carbon steel knife, this step is extremely important to prevent rust. Even a stainless steel blade can benefit from an external film of oil. Remember, stainless doesn't mean that steel won't rust. It just means that it's less likely to rust. If you don't believe me, then leave a low chromium stainless knife in the sheath for an extended period of time without wiping down the blade

and see what happens. When rust appears, don't say I didn't tell you so. In parts of the country that experience high humidity, a stainless blade with low chromium content (AUS-4, AUS-8, 420 J2, 3Cr13, 8Cr2MoV and ATS-34) can still rust if not properly protected.

Now that that the fixed-blade knife has been cleaned, dried and wiped with a film of protective oil, let's turn our attention to the sheath. Like the knife it safely carries, a leather sheath needs care. If the sheath has been tainted with blood or other body fluids, then a damp cloth can be used to wipe the leather clean. Particularly stubborn spots may take some time, but stay with it.

After the leather has dried, staining may have occurred. Not to worry. An application of leather preservative or conditioner will generally take care of the problem. If the leather has been tooled, an old toothbrush can be used to work the preservative into the tooling. Even if some staining remains, it won't harm leather. A slight stain, here and there, imparts character

To prevent the intrusion of moisture beneath the guard, place a drop of oil on either side of the blade where the blade tang and guard meet. (Image: Durwood Hollis)

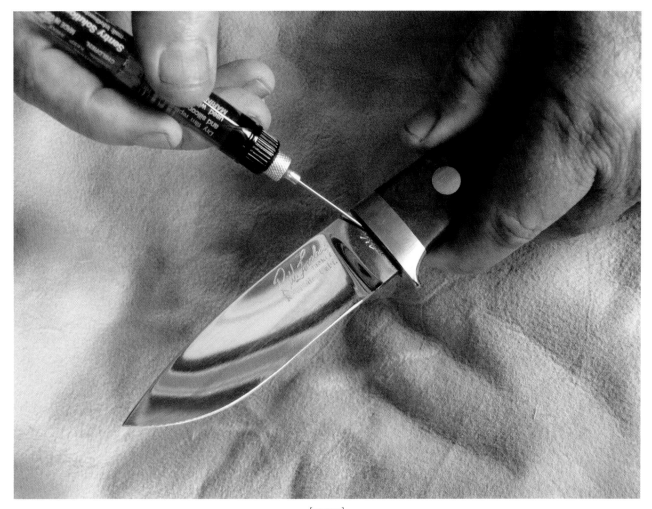

When the knife is clean and completely dry, wipe the blade and all exposed metal surfaces with a wiping cloth designed to protect against corrosion. In this instance, a foil-packed Tuf-Cloth from Sentry Solutions is used to lay down a non-toxic, dry film barrier. (Image: Durwood Hollis)

to a hunting knife sheath.

Long term storage of a knife in its sheath isn't recommended by some, particularly knife collectors. The chrome salts used in leather tanning processes can have a detrimental effect on blade steel. Since all of my knives are inspected and maintained on a regular basis, sheath storage has never been a problem. However, if you're concerned, then you can use a plastic slip cover to protect the sharpened edge and store your knife apart from the sheath. Even so, I still recommend at least an annual inspection. And don't keep your knife in an area where it is exposed to heat and humidity (for example, near a water heater). Both heat and humidity are enemies of blade steel and handle material.

Folding knives

We've discussed fixed-blade knives, so now it's time to move on to folders. Before dealing with the care process, however, let me mention a few words about folder safety. Since a folding knife blade moves into and out of handle containment, remember to keep your fingers out of the way of that movement cycle. More than once I've watched individuals close a folding knife without paying

Before you put your fixed-blade knife away, make sure you also clean the sheath. Wipe any external contaminants with a damp cloth, then use a small amount of leather conditioner to rehydrate and protect the leather. (Image: Durwood Hollis)

attention to where their fingers were in relation to the blade. A folding knife is every bit as sharp as a fixed-blade. When that sharp edge comes into contact with human flesh, the results are always less than favorable.

Many years ago at the Shooting, Hunting and Outdoor Trade (SHOT) show, I watched in horror as the sales director for a major production knife company accidentally closed a folding knife on all four fingers of his left hand. Initially, he didn't experience a lot of pain, but there was a lot blood and the incident necessitated a trip to a nearby emergency room. Many sutures later, his wound was repaired, but he was out of commission for quite awhile. Every time I think about the experience, it makes me shudder.

The new generation of one-hand opening folders can also present a problem. Even worse are those with some type of blade opening assistance mechanism. One of those beauties can spring open in an instant. While this might be a good thing when rapid deployment is needed, it can also be dangerous. One of the best things about using two hands to open a folder is that you maintain control of the knife. When only one hand is used, the same level of knife management isn't present.

When attending a knife show recently, I couldn't help but notice a man at one of the booths rapidly opening a knife with one hand. Actually, he was flipping the blade open in a rather forceful manner. You guessed it. It didn't take long before the knife flew out of his hand and landed with the blade tip imbedded into the top of his very expensive cowboy boots. He was fortunate. The blade tip missed injuring his foot, but the boots were beyond repair.

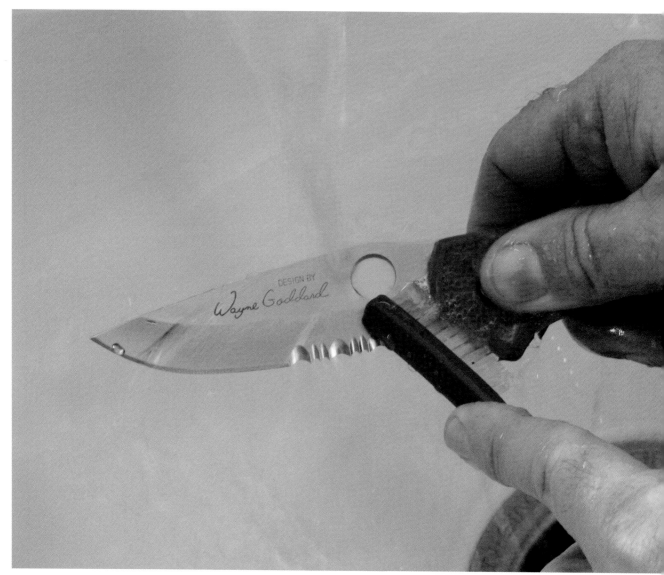

Cleaning a folding knife takes special care. Wash under hot water and use a small brush to scrub off any visible contaminants. (Image: Durwood Hollis)

While you may have seen someone on television or the movies flipping their knife open casually with one hand, remember that your knife isn't a movie prop and you're not a Hollywood stunt person.

Maintenance for a folding knife maintenance is more challenging than for a fixed-blade. To begin with, every folder has a main pin that attaches the blade tang to the knife frame. Both pin and tang are hidden, making them difficult to clean and maintain. Should the folding knife have a frame with a closed back, then the same thing is true of that location. Even an open-frame folder can present some cleaning difficulty. And if the folding knife has some type of blade locking mechanism, that presents another, even more complicated cleaning problem.

Once again, after field use wash the knife (blade and handle) with water. Shake off the excess moisture and wipe the blade as dry as possible. This primary care can eliminate most of the contaminants quickly and easily. The problem arises when small amounts of debris (animal fat, gristle, sand or dirt) remain within the inner workings of a folder. If the knife has an open frame, this is less likely to occur. However, special care must be give to a folder with a closed frame. When the frame is closed, it becomes very difficult to remove grit, grime and blood from within the blade containment channel.

To completely clean any folding knife, open or closed frame, you'll need to perform more than just a simple wash and wipe procedure. If the folder has a blade locking mechanism, either a back spring or locking liner mechanism, a thor-

When cleaning a folding knife, pay close attention to the area around the tang and lock mechanism. If grit, grime, blood or anything else remains behind, it can impede the function of these components. (Image: Durwood Hollis)

ough cleaning is even more important. When I return to camp or home, which ever comes first, my folding knife receives special attention.

First of all, the hot water and brush routine is an important beginning step. While the brush may loosen most of offending substances, with the hot water serving as a flushing agent, there can be enough garbage left behind to cause corrosion and impair blade movement over time. Moreover, if anything remains trapped in the blade locking mechanism, it can prevent complete lock engagement.

When an ever-dulling blade is pushed beyond performance parameters, a partially engaged locking mechanism can be overridden and fail without warning. A wise knife owner should never put too much confidence in a blade locking mechanism. Blade locks can and will fail. The primary reason for inadequate lock engagement is most likely contamination by an external substance. That is directly related to a lack of proper maintenance.

After cleaning a folder, it's a good idea to use some type of magnification instrument to carefully examine the blade containment channel in the frame, as well as the blade tang and lock mechanism (if any), to ensure that nothing remains behind. You'll be surprised at what the magnifier reveals. More than once, I've discovered a tiny film of dried blood or a microscopic piece of tissue hidden from view. For that reason, I keep a dental pick on hand to aid in cleaning.

When you've finished cleaning the knife, place a drop of oil on the tang and work the blade back and forth. This will allow the oil to seep in to coat the hidden portion of the tang and lubricate the main pin. If the blade is a bit stiff, some minor corrosion may have occurred. In most cases, a shot of penetrating oil will solve the problem.

After you've lubricated the axis upon which the blade revolves, wipe down the blade and all of the exposed metal components with an oil or silicone impregnated cloth. Oil is fine for use on metal, but it can have an adverse effect on many types of natural (wood, stag, etc.) handle materials. For this reason, some knife owners use silicone as protective barrier against moisture and chemical attacks.

Many folders are supplied with a belt case for ease of knife transport in the field. Leather, fabric, webbing and even hard thermoplastic material (Kydex) are

The blade containment channel within a folding knife frame is a place where lots of nasty stuff can hide. Make sure you clean this area thoroughly. (Image: Durwood Hollis)

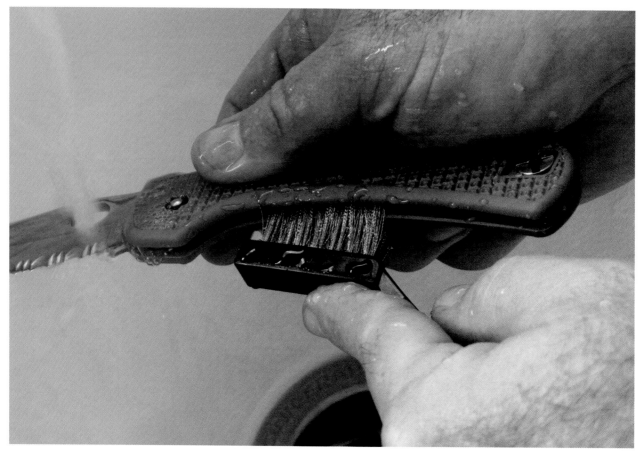

all used for case material. However, if the case has become damp, either from perspiration or ambient moisture, make sure it has time to dry out before returning the knife to containment. Dirt, mud and grime can usually be removed from a belt case with a damp brush. While fabric or webbing won't need any more attention than that, a leather case will need to be cared for just like a leather fixed-blade knife sheath. After cleaning the external surface of the leather, wipe it down with a leather preservation to prevent drying and cracking.

I've not experienced any problem with long-term (from one hunting season to another) storage of a folding knife in a belt case. Even so, I still recommend that every knife, fixed-blade or folding, be routinely examined at regular intervals, or at a minimum of once a year. While you may have thoroughly cleaned your knife, over time the protective nature of both oil and silicone can degrade, leaving the blade exposed to airborne moisture. This is particularly true if you reside in a saltwater coastal area, near large bodies of freshwater or where high humidity is prevalent.

Note to collectors

Many collect both fixed-blade and folding knives for personal enjoyment, as trading stock for profit, or even as a hedge against inflation. Keeping collectable knives in a pristine state can be challenging. Don't just store a knife away and forget about it. Rust demons can lurk everywhere. Nothing will go farther to ensure that your collection is protected against the ravages of environmental invectives than annual inspection and maintenance. This also applies to the sheath or belt case, the original packaging and sales receipt. I usually keep my collectable knives together, but apart from their original packaging and paperwork. This way, oil from the knife won't leak out and stain the box or paperwork. Protection of the entire knife package and its associated paperwork will guarantee that the collectable nature of your knife remains high.

Restoration

Some years ago, I found a small fixed-blade Western Cutlery hunting knife hidden in a crevice of a large rock outcropping. Apparently, the knife had been there for some time. The blade was covered with a patina of light rust and the leather handle was dried out and had shrunk away from the guard and pommel. There was

After cleaning a folder, dry it completely. Make sure you dry both the outside of the knife and the inside of the blade containment channel. (Image: Durwood Hollis)

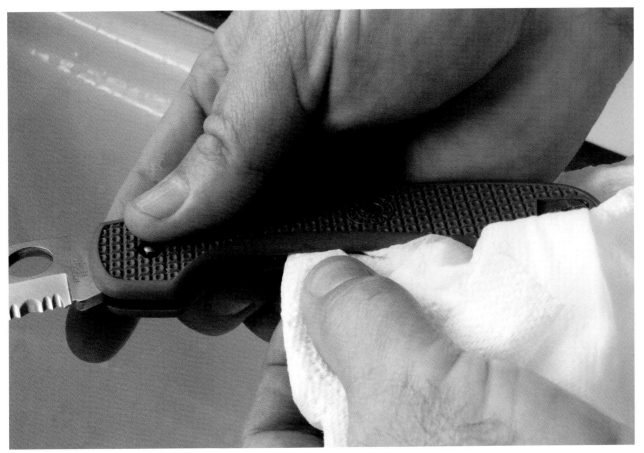

no sheath, so I assumed that the previous owner had left the knife behind after using it. Retrieving the knife from the crevice, I safely covered the blade edge with a piece of duct tape, and put it in my pack. Upon my return home, I decided to see if the knife could be restored to a semblance of working order.

First of all, the leather handle definitely needed some nourishment. I purchased a can of neatsfoot oil, poured it into a tall, narrow container, plunged the entire knife handle into the oil and left it there for several days. When the handle looked in better shape, I took it out of the oil and let it dry for a day or two. Afterwards, an additional application of leather conditioner made the handle look almost new again.

Next, I used some steel wool to remove the rust from the blade. It took a little time and some serious elbow grease, but the blade gleamed once again. I gave the single guard and the pommel a similar treatment, and

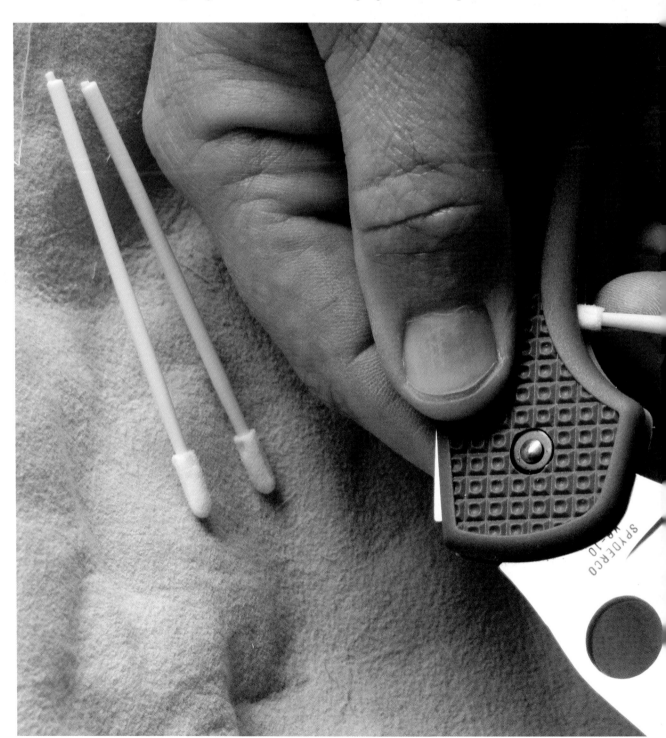

(below) The use of a cotton-tipped cleaning tool can help you clean the hard-to-reach areas within a folder. (Image: Durwood Hollis)

(right) A drop of oil in the tang area serves as both lubricant and corrosion inhibitor. Work the blade open and closed to ensure that the oil seeps into every crevice. (Image: Durwood Hollis)

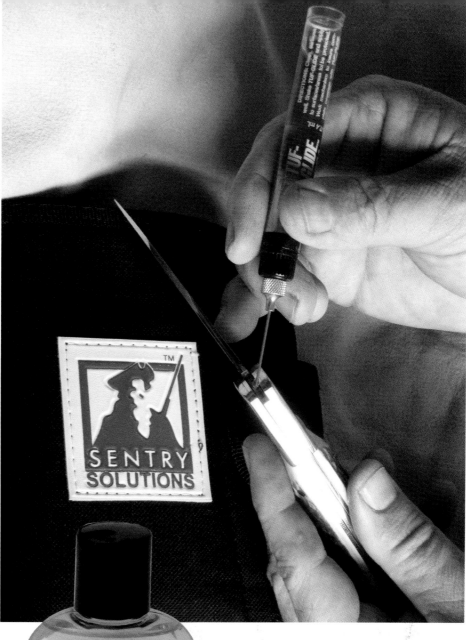

used metal polish to remove all of the stubborn stains. Finally, I sharpened the blade.

It hadn't taken much to restore the once-lost knife to its near original condition. A friend who works in leather made a new sheath for the knife and the following hunting season it was used to gut and skin a deer. While that old knife never made it back home to its original owner, I was able to put it back in service.

It's possible to restore some badly abused and mistreated knives to useful condition. Certainly, many collectors and knife enthusiasts have done just that. However, proper care and safe keeping can guarantee that any knife will continue to look good and perform properly for years to come.

Neatsfoot oil is used by many as a leather conditioner. However, there are many other choices. Remember that your leather knife sheath or belt case needs as much care as the knife itself. (Image: Durwood Hollis)

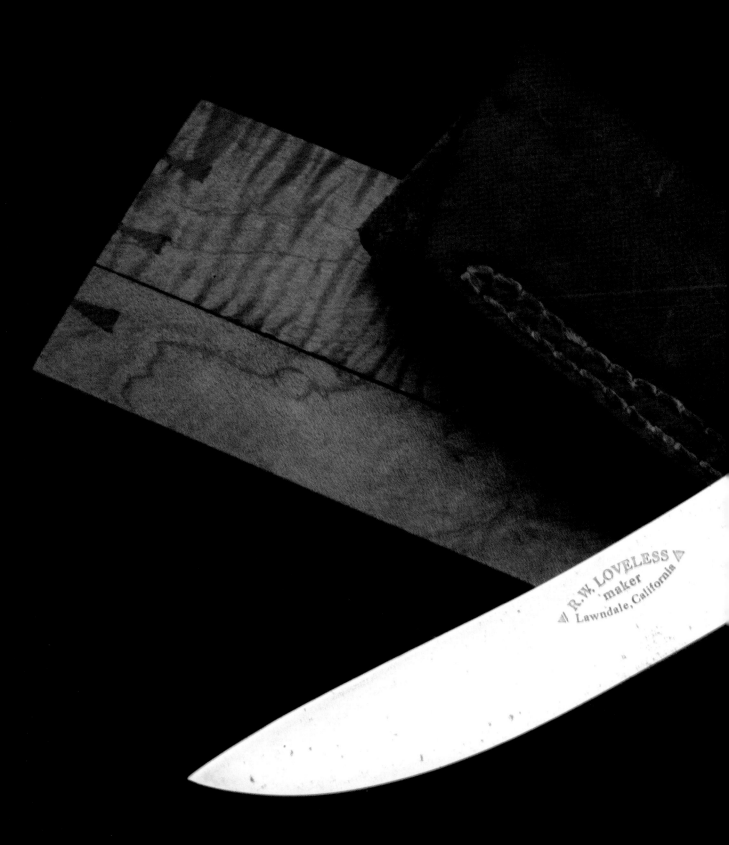

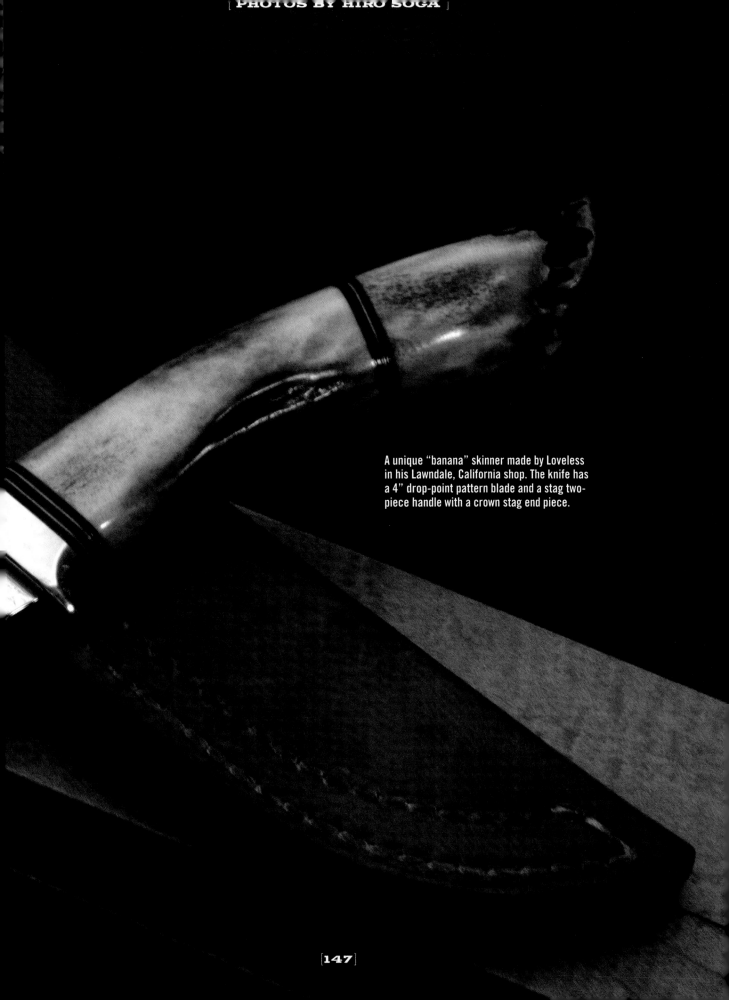

A unique "banana" skinner made by Loveless in his Lawndale, California shop. The knife has a 4" drop-point pattern blade and a stag two-piece handle with a crown stag end piece.

R. W. LOVELESS
maker
Lawndale, California

This utility knife features a 4-1/2" almost
straight blade, brass single guard and full
tang with stag handle scales.

(right) This Lawndale-made crooked skinner features a 4-1/2" extreme drop-point pattern blade, nickel-silver hilt and ebony handle. (left) This Love-less camp knife was crafted out of 1/4" stainless stock and features a 6-1/2" clip-point blade and full tang with an ebony handle.

Both of these knives are double guard fighters with Micarta handles. The knives differ only in that the bottom knife has a hidden tang.

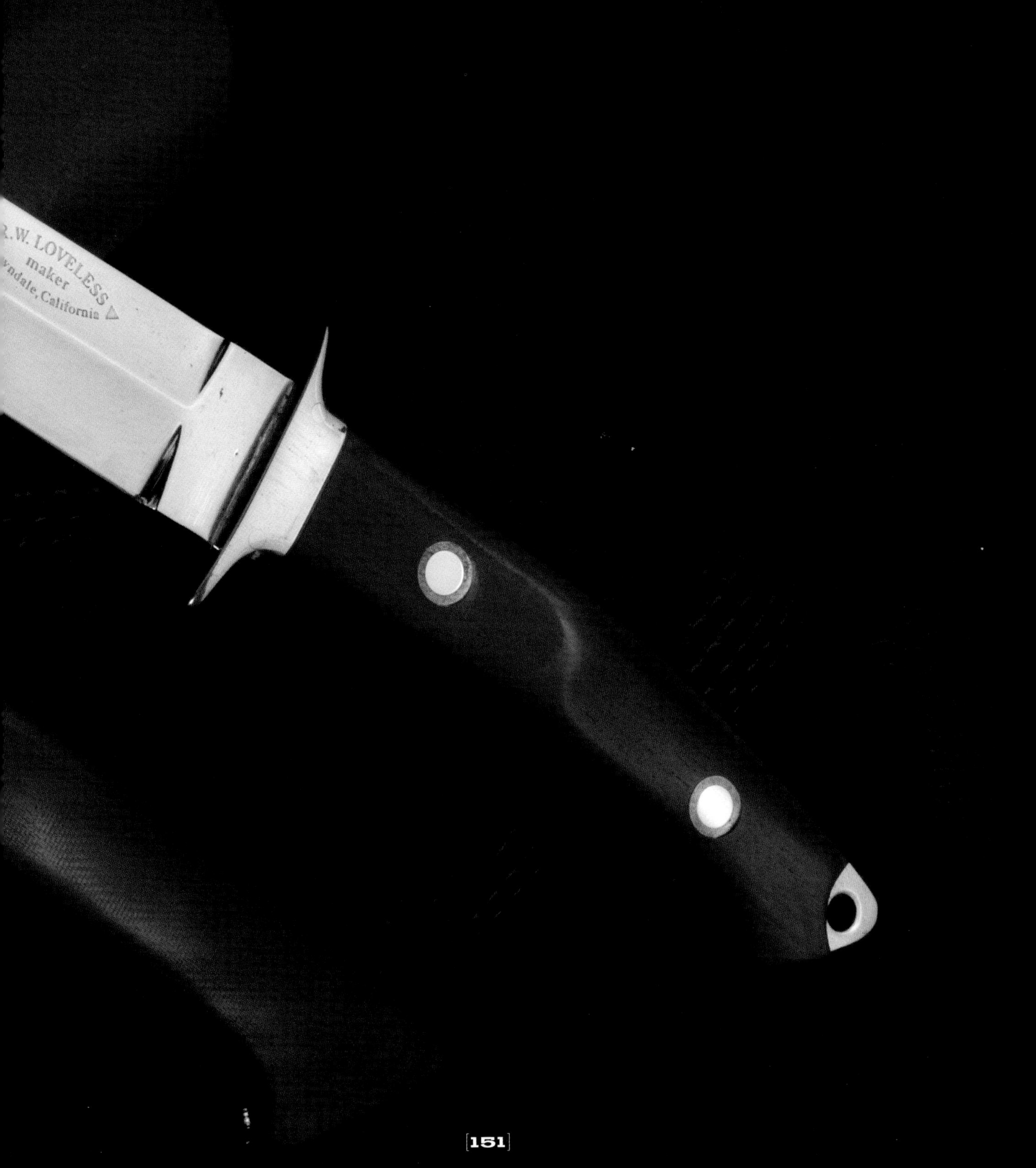

R.W. LOVELESS
maker
ndale, California △

CHAPTER NINE

Helping Hands

IN THE KNIFE SHOP
ASSISTANCE INCREASES PRODUCTIVITY
AND ENHANCES SAFETY

A full-partner in the business, Jim Merritt is as much a part of the production of Loveless knives as Bob is himself. (Image: Durwood Hollis)

It's safe to say that we've all needed a little assistance in our lives. My parents put my feet on the path of life. Many others taught me the necessary skills to stay on course. How well I remember my father involving me in whatever work he did around the house. At his side, I learned how to use tools to make and repair things.

Along the way, I learned that any handcrafting work is first born in the spirit. "You have to have it within you," my dad said. If there's no desire, then there's no ownership in the work. Someone else can share their desire and skill with you, but you have to be willing to learn, to achieve and to make it part of you.

When you've learned something of value, then it's important to share it with others. Asked about what kind of legacy he wanted to leave, Bob Loveless replied, "To have done the very best and to give something back."

(opposite) Producing knives in batches, like this outstanding Loveless fixed-blade, can be challenging for the individual knife builder. Those who want to replicate a particular design in sizeable numbers are always better off working with a partner. (Image: Hiro Soga / John Denton Collection)

Over the years, Bob has shared his knife making knowledge and skill with countless individuals. Some of that sharing came by way of magazine articles and books that outlined his thoughts and ideas on materi-

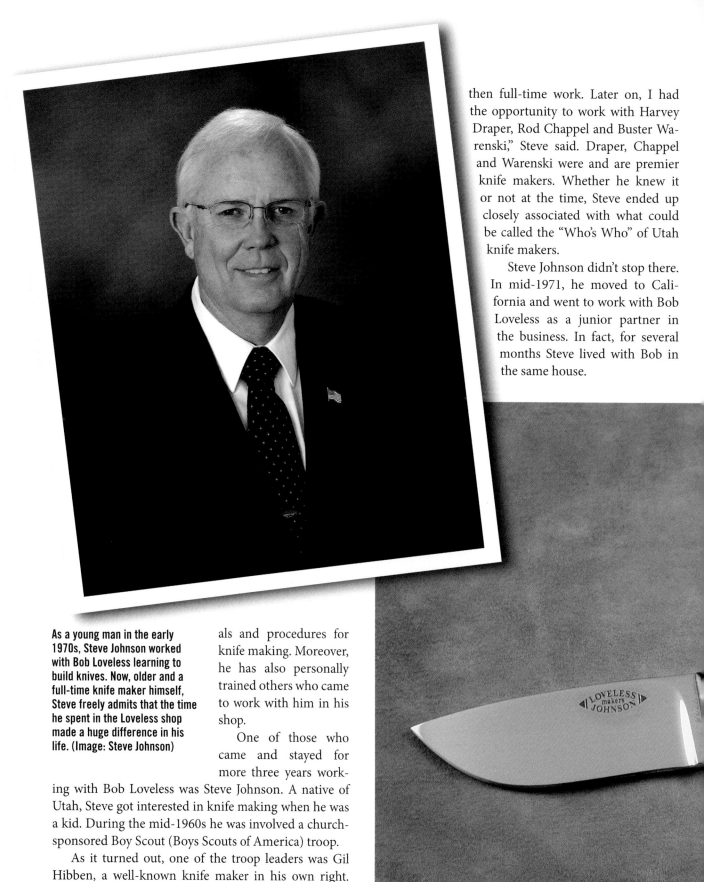

then full-time work. Later on, I had the opportunity to work with Harvey Draper, Rod Chappel and Buster Warenski," Steve said. Draper, Chappel and Warenski were and are premier knife makers. Whether he knew it or not at the time, Steve ended up closely associated with what could be called the "Who's Who" of Utah knife makers.

Steve Johnson didn't stop there. In mid-1971, he moved to California and went to work with Bob Loveless as a junior partner in the business. In fact, for several months Steve lived with Bob in the same house.

As a young man in the early 1970s, Steve Johnson worked with Bob Loveless learning to build knives. Now, older and a full-time knife maker himself, Steve freely admits that the time he spent in the Loveless shop made a huge difference in his life. (Image: Steve Johnson)

als and procedures for knife making. Moreover, he has also personally trained others who came to work with him in his shop.

One of those who came and stayed for more three years working with Bob Loveless was Steve Johnson. A native of Utah, Steve got interested in knife making when he was a kid. During the mid-1960s he was involved a church-sponsored Boy Scout (Boys Scouts of America) troop.

As it turned out, one of the troop leaders was Gil Hibben, a well-known knife maker in his own right. Hibben's specific assignment within the organization was that of the Explorer Scout Advisor. When Steve became an Explorer Scout, Hibben gave him and all of the other Explorers in the troop a knife making project.

"For me, the 'project' evolved into part-time and

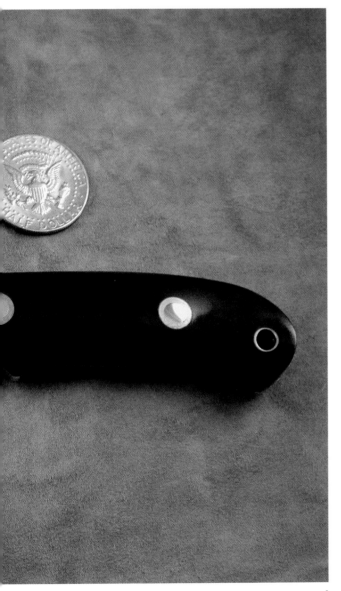

Pictured here is one of the few knives marked "Loveless-Johnson" still in existence. (Image: John Denton)

Those who know both Steve Johnson and Bob Loveless are amazed that the two got along so well. They seemed to be diametric opposites. Steve was actively involved with a religious organization that demanded a strict code personal conduct, which discouraged the use of profanity, alcohol and tobacco. In contrast, Bob was given to using ribald language, smoking cigarettes and enjoying an occasional alcoholic beverage.

When asked about that period of his life, Steve replied, "Bob had a lot of respect for the LDS (Latter-day Saint) church and that same respect transferred to me. He treated me like a son and we got along just fine."

During the time he worked at the Loveless shop, Steve learned a lot about knife construction integrity. He remembers that Bob was always searching for better materials, always striving for perfection. "Bob wanted his knives to be working tools, not just art objects. In his mind, practicality is art to Bob Loveless," Steve said.

From then to now, knife making has remained a constant presence in the life of Steve Johnson. He opened his own shop in 1975, and has been at it ever since (srj@mail.manti.com). One look at a Steve Johnson knife and the time he spent with Bob Loveless is clearly evident. And like Loveless, he strives to make every knife as flawless as possible.

There were other helpers, trainees and apprentices who came to the Loveless shop. Some came to watch and learn and others worked for a time with Bob. Always ready to share, Bob Loveless became a mentor to many. The clean lines of his designs and the purity of knife construction were irresistible to many would-be knife makers and cutlery purveyors alike.

In 1982, Jim Merritt came to the Loveless shop. Al-

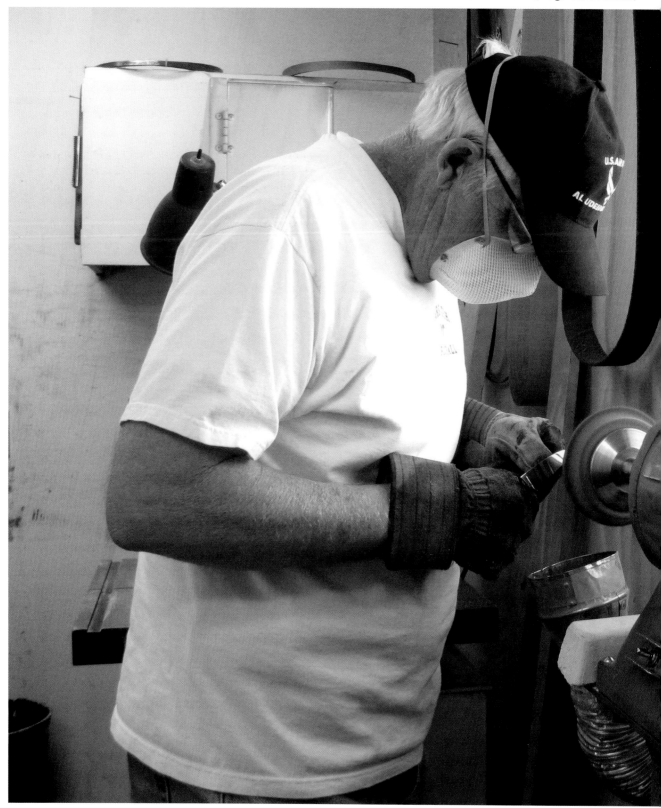

ready a full-time knife maker, Merritt regularly sold his knives at various shows. Jim had known Loveless for some time and they had struck up a friendship. "We used to hang out together at knife shows," Jim said. According to Merritt, "Bob asked me to come to the shop. He wanted me to look things over and make some suggestions. And I've been working with him ever since."

Obviously, the common interests of the two men became the springboard to an effective knife making partnership. "I started working for Bob as a junior partner, but became a full partner shortly thereafter," Jim said.

Jim Merritt is a native Californian. Born in Los Angeles in the mid-1930s, he soon moved with his family to Texas. His father owned property in the state that had originally been a Spanish land grant of some 48,000 acres. While in Texas, Jim's father, a private physician, served the medical needs of the surrounding area.

"In addition to being a doctor, my dad also wanted to be a gentleman farmer. However, that didn't work out. Mom and dad separated shortly after they arrived in Texas and finally divorced when I was about ten years old," Jim said.

When Jim's mother remarried, he returned with her and her new husband to the Los Angeles area shortly before the Korean conflict broke out. After graduating from high school, Jim attended college for two years and went on to a trade school to become a plumber. When his training was complete, he worked in that occupation for next 30 years.

In 1952, the movie "Iron Mistress," starring Alan Ladd and Virginia Mayo, was released. Alan Ladd played the famous Jim Bowie, with Virginia Mayo was his love interest. When Jim Merritt saw the movie he was fascinated by the large Bowie knife that Alan Ladd carried. Like many young men, we all have our heroes. Jim took an interest in knives, which eventually lead to a career in knife making.

Of course, Jim's budding interest in knives fit right into his family background in south Texas. To him, it seemed as though he was born to be involved with knives and knife making. Not only did the "Iron Mistress" movie stimulate this interest, Jim's grandfather had given him a small folding knife many years before. "I had to give granddad a penny before he gave me the knife. In this way, he felt that the knife wouldn't spoil our relationship," Jim said.

"In the 1960s, I bought World War II surplus knives and modified them to suit my needs. However, I really didn't get into knife making until 1970. I remember going to a gun show and seeing lots of knives that I wanted, but couldn't afford to have. Afterward, I went home with a determination to make my own knife," Jim said.

Jim had been a plumber and involved in construction for some time. Over the years he had gathered quite a supply of tools. This enabled him to make several small knives out of old files. The key to transition from amateur to professional knife maker, however, was his acquisition of an old Olympic square wheel grinder.

"That old grinder made knife making a lot easier. I became a part-time knife maker. My first few knives were given to my grandsons. And I continued to give knives to my friends and neighbors. When I had saturated everybody I knew with knives, I decided to start marketing my work to the public at large. All of my knives were fixed-blade models. And to date I've never made a folder," Jim stated.

By the dawn of the 1980s, Jim had become a full-time maker. He went to knife shows and set up a sales table. And he did some outside work grinding blades for the Cold Steel knife company. Then he joined up with Bob Loveless and has continued working with him in the Riverside, California, shop ever since.

Jim went on to say, "I learned Bob's knife making methods, especially how to produce knives in 20-30 piece batches. In reality, we

Jim Merritt, or "Jimmy" as Bob Loveless fondly refers to him, has worked with Bob Loveless for nearly 30 years. (Image: Durwood Hollis)

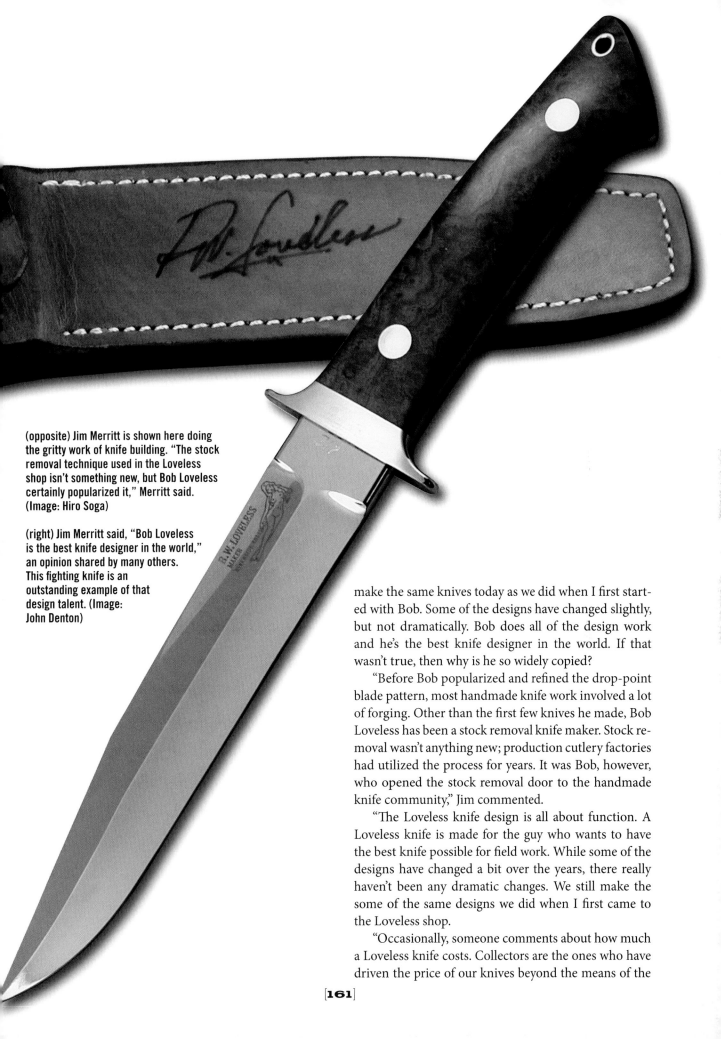

(opposite) Jim Merritt is shown here doing the gritty work of knife building. "The stock removal technique used in the Loveless shop isn't something new, but Bob Loveless certainly popularized it," Merritt said. (Image: Hiro Soga)

(right) Jim Merritt said, "Bob Loveless is the best knife designer in the world," an opinion shared by many others. This fighting knife is an outstanding example of that design talent. (Image: John Denton)

make the same knives today as we did when I first started with Bob. Some of the designs have changed slightly, but not dramatically. Bob does all of the design work and he's the best knife designer in the world. If that wasn't true, then why is he so widely copied?

"Before Bob popularized and refined the drop-point blade pattern, most handmade knife work involved a lot of forging. Other than the first few knives he made, Bob Loveless has been a stock removal knife maker. Stock removal wasn't anything new; production cutlery factories had utilized the process for years. It was Bob, however, who opened the stock removal door to the handmade knife community," Jim commented.

"The Loveless knife design is all about function. A Loveless knife is made for the guy who wants to have the best knife possible for field work. While some of the designs have changed a bit over the years, there really haven't been any dramatic changes. We still make the some of the same designs we did when I first came to the Loveless shop.

"Occasionally, someone comments about how much a Loveless knife costs. Collectors are the ones who have driven the price of our knives beyond the means of the average guy. That's one of the reasons that Bob has done some designing in collaboration with production cutlery firms. That way, a Loveless-designed knife is more affordable. However, the demand for Loveless knives has long exceeded our production capability. That being case, the price of an individual knife made in the Loveless shop will still be costly."

Since Bob Loveless has basically retired from active knife making, it's Jim Merritt who carries on the Loveless tradition. However, Bob does pitch in and help whenever and wherever he can. Regardless of whose hands craft the knife, every knife and sheath is a Bob Loveless design. And each one is made in his shop, with his tools and his oversight.

Teacher, mentor and friend, Bob Loveless has influenced a whole generation of knife makers. Those who have worked with him side-by-side know him best. Steve Johnson, who spent more than three years with Bob, told me recently that "Bob is a good man and the time I spent working with him changed my life."

Similarly, Jim Merritt, after working with Bob for nearly thirty years, said, "Bob Loveless is a true friend."

Knife making was and is Bob Loveless' life work. His knives, and those who provided the helping hands to craft them, are without equal.

This small fixed-blade hunter is another great example of the work that Bob Loveless and Jim Merritt have produced in the Riverside, California, shop. (Image: John Denton)

This is a prime example of the combined efforts of Bob Loveless and Jim Merritt. Their skill as knife makers is simply without peer. (Image: Durwood Hollis)

R.W. LOVELESS
maker
Riverside. Calif.

3/4

Only 36 knives bearing the Loveless-Parke logo were ever produced (Parke was an investor in Loveless's knifemaking business for a short period of time). This knife, made in 1967, is an example of that effort. The knife features a drop-point pattern blade, brass single guard and a stag handle with hidden tang construction.

Loveless & Parke
makers
Sierra Madre, Calif.

This full-tang, clip pattern utility knife was made by Loveless in 1962. It features a brass single guard and a hardwood handle.

This one-of-a-kind "hump back" (offset handle) fixed-blade was made in Lawndale, California, during the late 1960s. It combined a drop-point blade pattern, single guard and ivory handle. The cracks in the ivory, which are clearly visible, are the reason Loveless feels that it makes poor handle material.

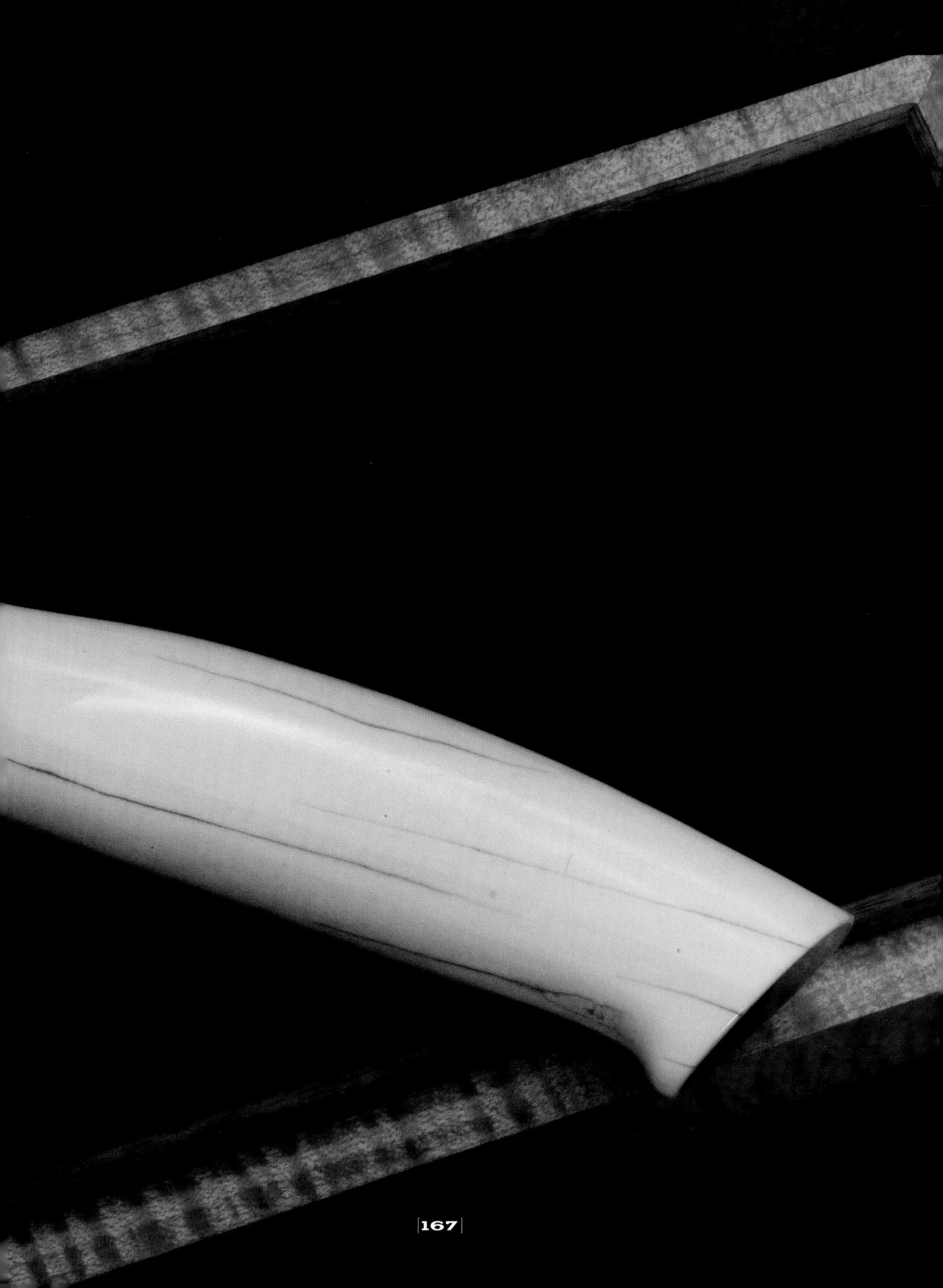

CHAPTER TEN

Resource Guide

WHERE TO FIND
WHAT YOU NEED

In the beginning, Bob Loveless couldn't buy the Randall knife he wanted, so he set out to make his own. A piece of automobile spring from a junkyard served as blade material. The rest of the components were scrounged up wherever he could find them. Not necessarily the best way to start out, but it worked. Today, those wanting to get into the knife making game have far greater access to supplies than Loveless did in the early 1950s.

A wide range of supply sources, from primary manufacturers to full-service knife supply purveyors, is available to anyone interested in building knives. At the outset, you may only want enough material to "get your feet wet." When you first start out, investing in a large quantity of material may not make the most sense. A good guideline is to start small and acquire supplies as the need arises.

At a minimum you'll need a few lengths of steel, material for guards and handle scales, pins, epoxy and various grades of abrasives. Some of this you may be

(opposite) To build a knife like this magnificient Loveless fixed-blade, you most likely won't find the necessary components at your local hardware store. However, a general knife supply shop can provide everything from blade steel to sheath leather. (Image: Hiro Soga/John Denton Collection)

able to find locally, but it's a lot easier to initially purchase what you need from a general knife supply retailer. If you really get into knife making, you'll need a larger amount of material. At that point, going direct to a specific manufacturer or distributor makes sense. However, you'll need to purchase a sizeable amount of material to realize any real savings.

Beginning knife makers often utilized blade steel that demands more experience, as well as a wider assortment of more specialized tools. Furthermore, many steels are not easily heat-treated in the home workshop. For these reasons, it's best to start using one of the simple alloys, like 01, A2 or the 5160, that was used in Chapter 3. While these steels aren't stainless, they're a lot easier to deal with than most of the stainless formulations, especially for someone new to blade work.

The same thing is true when it comes to handle material. Stag, desert ironwood and many other materials can be quite expensive. Rather than investing a sizeable sum in handle materials, try using something like Corian, Micarta or other synthetics that are more readily available, affordable and easier to work with. When you gain confidence with your abilities, you can always try your hand at something more exotic.

Many handle materials may be locally available. Scrap hardwood can be obtained from a woodworking shop at little or no cost. However, most wood will benefit from stabilization. If that isn't done, over time the wood can crack. Deer and elk antlers, as a result of your own hunting efforts or that of a friend, can also be found locally. Even though tropical deer antler material is a superior handle material, domestic deer antler can be used as scales, or even as handle material for narrow (hidden) tang knives. I've had good experiences with both North American deer and elk antler as knife handle material.

Knife shows can also be a source of inexpensive handle material, steel and other components. Many makers have surplus materials that they offer for sale at a show. I've purchased individual pieces of steel, pins, spacers, desert ironwood, horn and antler at knife shows for far less than it would have cost by mail or telephone order to an out-of-town supplier. This also saves the shipping costs. When you attend a knife show, be on the lookout for bargains in knife building materials.

(opposite) This beautiful Loveless hunter features stag handle material. Expect to pay a premium for the best stag, but there are other alternatives like red stag, elk horn and Pierre David deer horn. (Image: Hiro Soga / John Denton Collection)

From time to time, certain materials may be difficult to obtain. It that case, it's best to already have an alternative in mind. For example, good stag handle scale material has been almost impossible to obtain for some time, but red deer (European elk) antler can be used as an acceptable substitute. The same can be said about desert ironwood. Severe restrictions on gathering this material have resulted in decreased availability. In response, the cost for high quality desert ironwood handle material has risen dramatically. A new maker might want to consider using some other type of wood (stabilized) for handle scales.

Protect your investment with proper storage

Since acquiring knife building materials will necessitate an outlay of funds, protect your investment by using proper storage. Small components like pins, spacers and lanyard tubes can be stored in a multi-compartment plastic box designed to hold fishing tackle. Larger components will usually fit into plastic shoe boxes. You can store handle material, lengths of steel and other materials in these containers. Most are clear and come with a snap-on top.

In the Loveless shop, everything has its place. When a project begins, finding the right tools and components is never a problem. If you leave your tools and materials out on the work bench, expect them to go missing. When your wife or one of your children wants to use a hand tool, a can of lubricant, or something else to resolve whatever problem they're facing at the time, they often go straight to your supplies. You can nearly guarantee that whatever they've taken won't be returned to its original location.

Furthermore, small parts seem to intrigue children. Every child in my own home is always building something. Boys will make a toy gun out of whatever they can find in your shop and little girls seem to like hollow tubes (lanyard tubes) and other shiny stuff to make bracelets and necklaces. If you value your knife making gear, then store it properly until the next use. If you don't, then it just might sprout legs and walk away.

While you're at it, make sure you segregate and label everything. A label maker is a small investment that pays off in big, time-saving dividends. Looking for a particular component by going through countless bins, jars, coffee cans and whatever else you store your parts in is a serious time-waster and frustrating, especially when it all could have been avoided if you labeled each container.

The answer to all of this potential loss and confusion is proper storage. Personally, I'd keep everything under lock and key. That's the only way I've had success in holding on to my knife building tools and supplies. When too many people have access, problems arise. If knife building is important to you, then keep your shop clean, maintain your tools, and organize things so they are easily accessible.

Also, keep a running inventory of your supplies, including such things as epoxy, lubricants, thread-locking compound and whatever else you use regularly. It's disconcerting to be in the middle of a project and run out of something you really need. A good way to keep track of things is to write it all down and continually update that log.

All of these points about knife building components apply equally to the tools and materials used in sheath making. You don't want your leatherworking tools to be used inappropriately by others. Also, tanned leather can be scuffed, stained and damaged if handled incorrectly by those unfamiliar with proper leather care.

Business records

Many makers start out small, but those who have a knack for it can get into building knives in a big way. If and when you begin to move from hobbyist to a full-blown second job making knives, it's time to get serious about keeping track of your expenses and revenue. Remember, the government wants tax revenue. If you fail to collect sales tax, or pay income tax on your business venture, trouble awaits. Even if all of your work is home-based, depending on the particular jurisdiction where you reside, a business license might be necessary.

As you use various suppliers, keep a record of what they sell and each of your purchases. I maintain all of my contacts on index cards and categorize them according to their various specialties. Don't forget to indicate the name(s) and telephone extension(s) of those who you deal with. This will save you a lot of time. If you can't provide the name or extension of a particular contact, then you're apt to get bounced around from department to department or person to person.

Things in the business world are always in a state of flux. Don't get frustrated just because whoever it was you dealt with on your last purchase is no longer with the company. Get used to it. Find a supplier(s) that understands knife making needs and stick with them. If you continue building knives, over time you will develop a number of good contacts. Should a question or a specialized need arise, then you've already created a relationship with the "go to" person.

Bearing the blade stamp of "Loveless & Johnson," this dropped hunter has a number of component parts that must be flawlessly combined. Keep all of your knife building materials inventoried, that way you won't run out of something important when you need it. (Image: Hiro Soga / John Denton Collection)

Resources

The following listing of domestic knife making supply sources is assembled by category. The addresses, telephone numbers and websites were all current at the printing of this publication. Be advised that this listing is not all-inclusive. However, there are enough firms listed to provide the knife maker with several sources.

GENERAL KNIFE MAKING SUPPLIERS

These firms cater to knife makers and carry a wide range of materials including, but not limited to various steels, abrasives, handle materials, pins, rivets, drills, leather, knife kits and tools.

Alpha Knife Supply
(425) 868-5880
www.alphaknifesupply.com

Custom Kraft
12922-127th St., N., Largo, FL 34644
(813) 671-0661

Dixie Gun Works
P. O. Box 130, Union City, TN 38261
(731) 885-0700
www.dixiegunworks.com

Hawkins Knife Making Supplies
110 Buckeye Rd., Fayetteville, GA 30214
(770) 964-1023
www.hawkinsknifemakingsupplies.com

Jantz Supply
309 W. Main, Davis, OK 73030
(800) 351-8900
www.knifemaking.com

Knife and Gun Finishing Supplies
1972 Forest Ave., Lakeside, AZ 85929
(800) 972-1192
www.knifeandgun.com

Knife Kits
(877) 25-KNIFE
www.knifekits.com

Knives Plus
2467 Interstate 40 W, Amarillo, TX 79109
(806) 359-6202
www.knivesplus.com

Masecraft Supply Co.
Meriden, CT
(800) 682-5489
www.masecraftsupply.com

Sheffield Supply Co.
P.O. Box 741107, Orange City, FL 32774
(386) 775-6463
www.sheffieldsupply.com

Riverside Machine
201 W. Stillwell Ave., DeQueen, AR 71832
(870) 642-7643
www.riversidemachine.com

Texas Knife Maker's Supply
10649 Haddington, #180, Houston, TX 77043
(888) 461-8632
www.texasknife.com

Tru Grit Knife Making Supplies
760 E. Francis St., Unit N, Ontario, CA 91761
(909) 923-4116
(800) 532-3336
www.TRUGRIT.COM

Midwest Knife Maker Supply
42112 Kerns Dr., North Makata, MN 56003
www.USAKnifemaker.com

ABRASIVES

The knife maker will need several different types and grades of abrasive. Many of the following manufacturers specialize in abrasive belts, sheets, discs, rolls, buffing wheels and polishing compounds for the knife maker.

3M Abrasive Systems
223 6N-01 3M Center, St. Paul, MN
(612) 733-3702

Brownells
200 S. Front St., Montezuma, IA 50171
(641) 623-5401
www.brownells.com

G. L. Pearce Abrasive Co.
12771 Rt. 536, Punxsutawney, PA 15767
(814) 938-2379

Industrial Abrasives
642 N. 8th St., P.O. Box 14955
Reading, PA 19612
(800) 428-2222
www.industrialabrasives.com

Jackson & Lee
P.O. Box 699, Conover, NC 28613
(704) 464-1376

Norton Abrasives
1 New Bond St., P.O. Box 15008
Worcester, MA 01615
(508) 795-2183
www.ind.nortonabrasives.com

Red Hill Corp.
P. O. Box 4234, Gettysburg, PA 17325
(800) 822-4003
www.supergrit.com

Sandusky Abrasives
730 E. Washington St., Sandusky, OH 44870
(419) 625-0150

Stephen Bader & Co.
10 Charles St., P. O. Box 297
Valley Falls, NY 12185
(518) 753-4456
www.stephenbader.com

BLADE SMITH SCHOOLS

Class instruction on forging blades.

Moran School of Bladesmithing
Contact: Ms. Regina Fant
ABS School Director, Texarkana College
2500 N. Robison Rd., Texarkana, TX 75501
(903) 838-4541
rfant@texarkanacollege.edu

CARVING & CARVING TOOLS

These firms specialize in carving tools and power carving equipment.

Riverside Machine
201 W. Stillwell Ave., DeQueen, AR 71832
(870) 642-7643
www.riversidemachine.net

Ultra Speed Products
29844 – 24th Ave., SW,
Federal Way, WA 98023
(800) 373-0707
www.turbocarver.co

Wood Carver's Supply
P.O. Box 7500, Englewood, FL 34295
(800) 284-6229
www.woodcarverssupply.com

DISPLAY CASES

Specialty display cases for knife makers. While prefabricated cases are available, several of these firms are willing to customize a case for a particular need.

Bill's Custom Cases
(541) 727-7223
www.billscustomcases.com

Dorris Wood Creations
11845 E. 310 S., Lagrange, IN 46761
(260) 336-0764
www.dorriswoodcreations.com

Jomar Display Cases
13410 Morgan Dr., Splendora, TX 77372
(281) 399-1891
www.jomardisplay.com

HANDLE MATERIALS

These manufacturers carry a wide assortment of wood, stag, horn, bone, ivory and other materials for knife handle scales, hidden tang knife handles, inlays, etc.

Arizona Ironwood
(602) 283-4007
www.arizonaironwood.com

Boone Trading Co.
P.O. Box 669, Brinnon, WA 98320
(360) 796-4330
www.boonetrading.com

Cains Outdoor, Inc.
1832 Williams Hwy., Williamstown, WV 26187
(800) 445-1776
www.cainsoutdoor.com

Culpepper & Co.
P. O. Box 690, 8285 Georgia Rd., Otto, NC 28763
(828) 524-6842
www.knifehandles.com

Donald Fields
790 Tamerlane St., Deltona, FL 32725
(386) 532-9070
donaldfields@earthlink.net

Earl Mann, Fosslized & Mammoth Ivory
5532 Merry Oaks Rd., The Plains, VA 20198
(540) 349-2518
www.eaglestoneone.com

Elen Hunting & Importing
50 Battlehill Ave., Springfield, NJ 07081
(973) 379-5296
www.elenhunting.com

Gallery Hardwoods,
Eugene, OR 97403
www.galleryhardwoods.com

Gilmer Wood Co.
2211 N.W. St. Helens Rd.
Portland, OR 97210
(503) 274-1271
www.gilmerwood.com

Giraffe Bones Inc.
3052 Isim Rd., Norman, OK 73026
(888) 804-0683
www.giraffebone.com

IJ Trade Inc. Mammoth Ivory
(818) 486-4629
www.ijtrade.com/mammoth

It's a Burl
24025 Redwood Hwy., P.O. Box 3156
Kerby, OR 97531
(541) 592-5071
itsaburl@hotmail.com

Johnson Wood Products
34897 Crystal Rd.
Strawberry Point, IA 52076
(563) 933-6504
www.johnsonwoodproducts.com

Masecraft Supply Co.
254 Amity St., Meriden, CT 06450
(800) 682-5489
www.masecraftsupply.com

Nelson Woodworking
601 W. Main Rd., Little Compton, RI 02827
(401) 635-4733
www.johnsonwoodworking.com

Oso Famoso
P.O. Box 654, Ben Lomond, CA 95005
(831) 336-2343
www.osofamoso.com

Wild Boar Blades
P.O. Box 328, Toutle, WA 98649
(360) 274-7069
www.wildboarblades.com

HEAT TREATING

Many firms offer this service in conjunction with other products and services. However, those listed below are specialists in the process.

Bob Holt (Pacific Heat Treat)
1238 Birchwood Dr., Sunnyvale, CA 94089
(408) 736-8500
www.doug@pacificheattreat.com

Bodycote Thermal Processing
710 Burns St., Cincinnati, Ohio 45204
(513) 921-2300
www.bodycote.com

Paul Bos Heat Treating
660 S. Lochsa St. Post Falls, ID 83854
(208) 262-0500 x211
paulbos@buckknives.com

Peter's Heat Treating
P.O. Box 624, 215 Race St.
Meadville, PA 13665
(814) 333-1782
www.petersheattreat.com

Progresssive Heat Treating Co.
2802 Charles City Rd., Richmond, VA 23231
(804) 545-0010
www.pecqears.com

Richard Bridwell
801 Milford Ch. Rd., Taylors, SC 29687
(803) 895-1715

Texas Heat Treating
155 Texas Ave., P.O. Box 1117, Round Rock,
TX 78680
(512) 255-5884
www.texasheattreating.com

INSTRUCTIONAL DVDS

It's been said that "a picture is worth a thousand words." That being true, then the beginning knife maker can learn more from an instructional DVD than reading about the same procedures. At the very least, a DVD is another asset in your library of knife making materials.

Ed Fowler's Knife Talk
(307) 856-9815
www.edfowler.com

Center Cross Instructional Videos
851 House St., Fort Worth, TX 76103
(817) 496-3414
www.CCInstructionalVideos.com

Paladin Press
7077 Winchester Circle, Boulder, CO 80301
(800) 392-2400
www.paladin-press.com

ENGRAVING & ENGRAVING TOOLS

Engraving service and easy-to-use metal engraving tools designed for knife makers.

Baron Engraving
62 Spring Hill Rd., Trumbull, CT 06611
(203) 452-0515
www.baronengraving.com

Billy Bates Engraving
2302 Wintrop Dr., Decatur, AL 35603
(205) 355-3690
www.angelfire.com/al/billbatesbbrn@aol.com

Glenco Corp/GRS Tools
900 Overlander Rd., Emporia, KS 66801
(620) 343-1084
glendco@glenco.com

Henry A. Evers
72 Oxford St., Providence, RI 02905
(800) 55-EVERS
www.henryaevers.com

Lindsay Engraving & Tools
3714 W. Cedar Hill, Kearney, NE 68845
(308) 236-7885
www.AirenGraver.com

Paragrave
517 S. Commerce Rd., Orem, UT 84058
(800) 624-7415
www.profitablehobbies.com

Scott Plinkington
P. O. Box 97, Monteagle, TN 37356
(931) 924-3400
www.learntoengrave.com

KNIFE KITS

Easy-to-assemble and finish knife kits for the hobbyist knife builder.

Atlanta Cutlery
2147 Gees Mill Rd., Box 839, Conyers, GA 30013
(770) 922-7500
www.atlantacutlery.com

Crazy Crow Trading Post
P.O. Box 857, Pottsboro, TX 75076
(800) 786-6210
www.crazycrow.com

Damascus USA
149 Deans Farm Rd., Tyner, NC 27980
www.damascususa.com

House of Blades
6451 NW Loop #20, Ft. Worth, TX 76135
(817) 237-7721
www.houseofbladestexas.com

Jantz Supply
309 W. Main, Davis, OK 73030
(800) 351-8900
www.knikfemaking.com

Knife & Gun Finishing Supplies
P.O. Box 458, Lakeside, AZ 85929
(928) 537-8877
www.knifeandgun.com

Knife Kits.com
P.O. Box 215, Haralson, GA 30229
(877) 255-6433
www.knifekits.com

Linville Knife & Tool
5645 Murray Rd., Winston-Salem, NC 27106
(336) 923-2062
www.linvilleknifeandtool.com

Masecraft Supply
254 Amity St., Meriden, CT 06450
(800) 682-5489
www.masecraftsupply.com

NorthCoast Knives
17407 Puritas Ave., Cleveland, OH 44135
(216) 265-8678
www.northcoastknives.com

Texas Knifemakers Supply
10649 Haddington, #180, Houston, TX 77043
(713) 461-8632
www.texasknife.com

Universal Agencies
4690 S. Old Peachtree Rd. #C, Norcross, GA 30071
www.knifesupplies.com

Wood Lab
P.O. Box 222, 2416A Chicago Dr.
Hudsonville, MI 49426
(616) 322-5846
www.woodlab.biz

LEATHER & LEATHER SHEATHS

These firms offer leather in various grades/color/types for sheath work, custom quality leather sheaths made to knife maker's specifications, leather working tools and finishing materials.

Charles Clemens
1741 Dallas St., Aurora, CO 80016
(303) 364-0403
www.jacksandsaps.com

Cow Catcher Leatherworks
3006 Industrial Dr., Raleigh, NC 27609
(919) 83308262
www.cowcatcher.us

Dave's Custom Leather
1596 Boise St., Rathdrum, ID 83858
(208) 687-0150

El Paso Saddlery
2025 E. Yandell, El Paso, TX 79903
(915) 544-2233
www.epsaddlery.com

Hunter Co.
3300 W. 71st St., Westminister, CO 80030
(303) 427-4626
www.huntercompany.com

Jim Layton Leather
2710 Gilbert Ave., Portsmouth, OH 45662
(614) 353-6179

Jim Riney Leather
6212 S. Marion Wy., Littleton, CO 80121
(303) 794-1731

Leather Crafters & Saddlers
222 Blackburn St. Rhinelander, WI 54501
(715) 362-5393
www.leathercraftersjournal.com

Muir & McDonald Co., Tanners
P.O. Box 136, Dallas, OR 97338
(800) 547-1299
MuirMcDonald@aol.com

Oklahoma Leather Products
500-26th NW, Miami, OK 74354
(918) 542-6651
www.oklahomaleatherproducts.com

Raine Inc.
6401 S. Madison Ave., Anderson, IN 46013
(800) 826-5354
www.raineinc.com

Rowe's Leather
3219-Hwy. 29 S., Hope, AR 71801
(870-) 777-8216
www.rowesleather.com

Schrap Custom Leather Sheaths
7024 W. Well St., Wauwatosa, WI 52313
(414) 771-6472
knifesheaths@aol.com

Tandy Leather Co.
900 SE Loop 820, Fort Worth, TX 76140
(817) 872-3200
www.tandyleatherfactory.com

Treestump Leather
443 Cave Hill Rd., Waltham, ME 04605
(207) 584-3000
www.treestumpleather.com

Walt Whinnery Custom Leather
1947 Meadow Creek Dr., Louisville, KY 40218
(502) 458-4361

Wolf's Knives
627 Cindy Ct., Aberdeen, MD 21001
(410) 272-2959
wolfsknives@comcast.net

LEATHER POWER STITCHING EQUIPMENT
Heavy-duty sewing machines made to handle thick scabbard and sheath materials.

Artisan Stitcher
(888) 838-1408
www.artisansew.com

Tippmann Industrial Products
Ft. Wayne, IN
(866) 286-8046
www.tippmannindustrial.com

LUBRICANTS
Lubricants for tools, machinery and folding knives.

Clenzoil Worldwide
1434 Hobbs St., Tampa, FL 33619
(813) 662-6454
www.clenzoil.com

Sentry Solutions
P.O. Box 214, 5 Souhegan St.
Wilton, NH 03086
(800) 546-8049
www.sentrysolutions.com

Tai Lubricants
P. O. Box 1579, Hockessin, DE 19707
(302) 326-02300
nyoil@aol.com

White Lightning
1545-5th Industrial Ct., Bay Shore, NY 11706
(631) 206-1674 x207

SHARPENERS
Edge establishment and restoration tools for the knife maker or user.

A.G. Russell Knives
2900 S. 26th St., Roger, AR 72758
(800) 255-9034
www.agrussell.com

AccuSharp
205 Hickory Creek Rd.
Marble Falls, TX 78654
(830) 693-6111
www.accusharp.com

Dan's Whetstone Co.
418 Hilltop Rd., Pearcy, AR 71964
(501) 767-1616
www.danswhetstone.com

Diamond Machine Technology
85 Hayes Memorial Dr.
Malborough, MA 01752
(800) 666-4368
www.dmtsharp.com

Edgecraft Corp (Chef's Choice)
825 Southwood Rd., Avondale, PA 19311
(800) 342-3255
www.chefschoice.com

Edgemaker Co.
2000 Fairwood Ave., Columbus, OH 43207
(614) 458-1880
www.edgemaker.com

Edge Pro Sharpening Systems
P. O. Box 95, Hood River, OR 97031
(541) 387-2222
www.edgeproinc.com

EZE-LAP Diamond Products
3572 Arrowhead Dr., Carson City, NV 89706
(775) 888-9500
www.eze-lap.com

GATCO Sharpeners
P.O. Box 600, Getzville, NY 14068
(716) 877-2200
www.gatcosharpeners.com

Hall's Arkansas Oilstones
3800 Amity Rd., Pearcy, AR 71964
(501) 525-8595
www.hallsproedge.com

Lansky Sharpeners
P. O. Box 50830, Henderson, NV 89016
www.lansky.com

McGowan Manufacturing Co.
4854 N. Shamrock Pl., #100
Tucson, AZ 85705
(520) 219-0884
www.mcgowanmfg.com

Microedge Systems
136 Marycrest Ln., W. Seneca, NY 14224
(716) 826-0802

Norton Abrasives
1 New Bond St., P.O. Box 15008
Worcester, MA 01616
(508) 795-2183
www.ind.nortonabrasives.com

Oregon Abrasives
12345 NE Sliderberg Rd.
Brush Prairie, WA 98606
(360) 892-1142

Razor Edge Systems
303 N. 17th Ave., Ely, MN 55731
(218) 365-6419
www.razoredgesystems.com

Sharp'nr Co.
3503 W. Oak, P.O. Box 1369
Palestine, TX 75801
(903) 729-7831
sales@aladdinsharpener.com

Smith's Abrasives
1700 Sleepy Hollow Rd.
Hot Springs, AR 71901
(800) 221-04156
www.smithedge.com

Spyderco
820 Spyderco Wy., Golden, CO 80403
(800) 525-7770
www.spyderco.com

The Edge Maker Co.
2000 Fairwood Ave., Columbus, OH 43207
(800) 532-EDGE
www.edgemaker.com

The Epicurean Edge
107 Central Wy., Kirkland, WA 98033
(425) 889-5980
www.epicureanedge.com

The Ultimate Edge
3435 Ocean Park Blvd, #112, Santa Monica,
CA 90405
(800) 988-5946
www.theultimateedge.com

Tru Hone Corp.
1721 N.E. 19th Ave., Ocala, FL 34470
(800) 237-4663
www.truhone.com

Warthog Sharpeners
P.O. Box 150398, Austin, TX
(877) 719-0123
www.warthogsharp.com

STAMPS

Custom manufactured blade stamps, made to fit individual needs, are available from these manufacturers.

A.A. White Co.
444 Washington St., Providence, RI 02901
(401) 453-4300

Buckeye Engraving
(330) 677-5685
www.steelhandstamps.com

Harper Mfg.
3050 Westwood Dr., Las Vegas, NV 89109
(800) 776-8407
www.harpermfg.com

Henry A. Evers Corp.
72 N. Oxford St., Providence, RI 02905
(401) 781-4767, (800) 55-EVERS
www.HenryAEvers.com

STEEL

The manufacturers listed below are domestic producers of sheet and plate carbon and stainless steel products specifically for the cutlery industry. Some will laser cut steel to your specifications.

Admiral Steel
4152 West 123rd. St., Alsip, IL 60803
(800) 323-7055
www.admiralsteel.com

Allegheny Ludlum Steel Corp.
100 Six PPG Pl., Pittsburg, PA 15222
(412) 394-2800

Armco
17400 State Rt. 16, Coshocton, OH 43812
(800) 422-4422

Avesta Sheffield
425 N. Martingale Rd., #2000, Schaumburg, IL60173
(708) 517-4050

Niagara Specialty Metals
(716) 52-5552
www.nsm-ny.com

Chad Nichols Damascus
(662) 538-5966
www.chadnicholsdamascus.com

Crazy Crow Damascus
P. O. Box 847 D-32, Pottsboro, TX 75076
(800) 786-6210
www.crazycrow.com

Crucible Materials Corp.
575 State Fair Blvd., Syracuse, NY 13201
(800) 365-1168
www.crucible.com

Egoundstock Knife Steels
(516) 942-4447
www.egroundstock.com

Latrobe Specialty Steel
2626 Ligonier St., Latrobe, PA 15650
(724) 532-6519
www.labrobesteel.com

PPC Specialty Metals
1504 Miller St., Monroe, NC 28110
(800) 323-2671
www.toolsteel-specialtymetals.com

Stamascus Knife Works
24255 N. Fork River Rd. Abingdon, VA 24210
(276) 944-4883
www.stamascus-knife-works.com

Trans World Alloys
334 E. Gardena Blvd, Gardena, CA 90248
(800) 217-8777
www.twalloys.com

TITANIUM

Titanium sheet, rod, and finished clips for knife making.

Halpern Titanium
(888) 283-8627
www.HalpernTitanium.com

TOOLS

While most hand tools can be obtained at local sources, industrial quality power tools, hydro/ laser cutters, grinders, forges and many more specialized tools for knife makers are available from these providers.

Amburr Industries
337 Conifer Dr. N., Providence, RI 02904
(401) 353-0113

American Seipmann Corp.
65 Pixley Industrial Parkway, Rochester, NY 14624
(585) 247-1640
www.seipmann.com

Beaumont Metal Works
1473 Showcase Dr., Columbus, OH 43212
(614) 291-8876
www.beaumontmetalworks.com

Berger
44160 Plymouth Oaks Blvd., Plymouth, MI 48170
(734) 414-0402
www.berger.com

Blacksmith's Depot
100 Daniel Ridge R., Candler, NC 28715
(828) 667-8868
www.blacksmithsdepot.com

Burr King
1220 Tamara Ln., Warsw, MO 65355
(800) 621-2748
www.burrking.com

Centaur Forge
117 N. Spring St. Burlington, WI 53105
(800) 666-9175
www.centaurforge.com

Evenheat Kiln, Inc.
6949 Legion Rd., Caseville, MI 48726
(989) 856-2281
www.evenheat-kiln.com

Jancy Engineering
2735 Hickory Grove Rd., Davenport, IA 52804
(563) 391-1300
www.jancy.com

LMS Stamping
1209 W. LeHigh St., Behleham, PA 18018
(610) 867-1401
www.lmsstamping.com

Midwest Knifemakers Supply Grinder Plans
www.USAknifemaker.com

NC Tool Co. Inc.
6133 Hunt Rd., Pleasant Grove, NC 27313
(336) 674-5654
www.nctoolco.com

Paragon Industries
2011 S. Town East Blvd., Mesquite, TX 75149
(800) 876-4328
www.paragonweb.com

Reba's Enterprises Hollow Grinders
419 Warner St., NW, Huntsville, AL 35805
(256) 837-0308

Speed Cut Grinders
Box 399, Ephraim, UT 84627

Tormach
www.tormach.com

WMH Tool Group
2420 Vantage Dr., Elgin, IL 60123
(888) 804-7129
www.wmhtoolgroup.com

WOOD STABILIZATION
Most woods will benefit from stabilization. The process prevents cracking and other changes due to humidity.

Wood Lab
P. O. Box 222, Hudsonville, MI 49426
(616) 322-5846
www.woodlab.biz

This Loveless skinner, made in Lawndale, California, during the early 1960s, features a full length tang, hidden attachment pins and a hardwood handle.

WOOD/LOVELESS
MK 4 TITANIUM
MODEL #001

WOOD/LOVELESS
makers
venice · california

WOOD/LOVELESS
makers
venice · california

WOOD/LOVELESS
MK 4 ALUMINUM
SAMPLE-1 ONLY MADE

Made at the time Loveless collaborated with knifemaker Barry Wood. Wood had a shop in Venice, California, and had developed an unusual folding knife mechanism. These knives are extremely rare examples of unique Loveless-Wood folders.

Made in 1974, during the three and one-half year period that Steve Johnson worked with Bob Loveless, this skinner features a sculpted maroon Micarta handle. Johnson went on to be an accomplished knife maker and now resides in Manti, Utah.

Shown here in cross section (top) is a Loveless skinning
knife that clearly exhibits how the hidden tang is done.
The smaller utility knife (bottom), with a 2-1/2" blade and
stag handle, is one of a kind and was made by Loveless
when he had a home/shop in Lawndale, California.

R.W. LOVELESS
maker
Lawndale, California

Afterword

It has been a tough day in the field. Hunting in Wyoming's high desert country on foot is never easy, but trekking through a maze of narrow honeycombed canyons is about as hard as it can get. However, success had come late in the morning when a nice mule deer buck exploded out of the sage. Running shots can be challenging but, on this occasion, everything came together.

The rest of morning into early afternoon was spent working on the animal. I had to stop a couple of times and touch up the edge of my knife, but otherwise everything went as expected. After finishing with the carcass, I loaded my pack with fresh venison, strapped the antlers on top and headed back to my truck.

The day was well spent by the time I reached the trail head. While loading everything in the truck, a couple of hunters pulled along side in their own vehicle. During the course of exchanging pleasantries, one of guys saw the knife on my belt. The R. W. Loveless signature on the sheath clearly indicated what lay within.

"You carry a Loveless knife! I though they were all collector's items," he said.

When I reassured him that my knife was a functional tool, not something that lay gathering dust in a collection, he seemed shocked. Since collectors have pushed the cost of Loveless knives beyond reason, I could understand his amazement that someone would actually put one to use.

Bob Loveless got into knife making to produce a functional edged tool, and tools are made to use. It's not unusual for me to get elbow-deep into a game care project with my Loveless knife. Countless others use their Loveless creations in a similar manner.

"Nothing pleases me more than when a customer calls or writes to tell me about how well one of my knives worked for them in the field," Bob said.

Obviously, building knives has been and continues to be more than a job for Bob Loveless. It's the creation of something that only he can see within a piece of steel. Like a sculptor who frees from stone what lies within, Loveless is a life-giver to the knife hidden inside of a larger steel matrix.

Hopefully, this book will encourage you to step out and create your own knives. No doubt, in the beginning you will emulate what has already been done. In time, however, your own gift will emerge. Whatever it is, seek it and you'll find it. Bob Loveless did, and his work is a testimony to that desire.

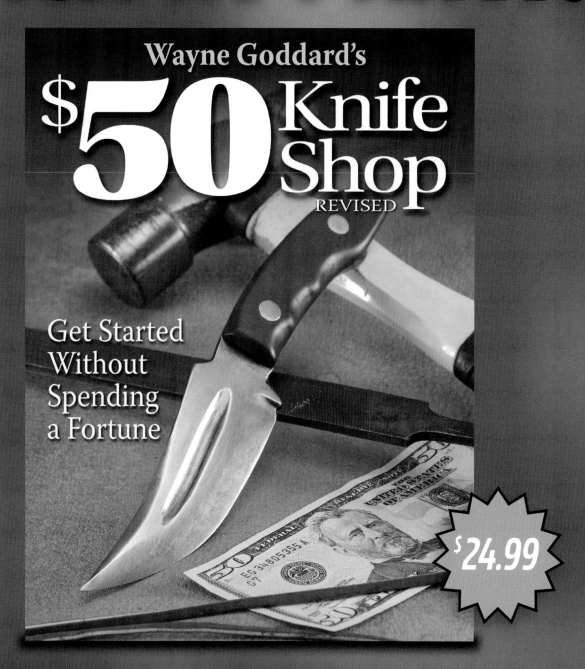